EAT UP!

CHARLES CAMPION

Kyle Cathie Limited

First published in Great Britain in 2010 by
Kyle Cathie Limited
23 Howland Street
London W1T 4AY
general.enquiries@kyle-cathie.com
www.kylecathie.com

10 9 8 7 6 5 4 3 2 1

ISBN 978-1-85626-856-1

A Cataloguing in Publication record for this title is
available from the British Library.

Designer: Jonathan Gray, gray318
Editor: Judith Hannam
Proofreader: Abi Waters
Copyeditor: Deborah Stottor
Production: Gemma John

Printed and bound in Slovenia by Gorenjski Tisk

CONTENTS

INTRODUCTION

WHY, I HEAR YOU ASKING, do we need yet another book about British food? And it's not a bad question. As someone who is not only passionate about food and cooking but also makes his living writing about it, I am only too aware of the flood of books on the subject: fat historical books about bygone dishes with lovingly updated recipes for leaden steamed puddings; thin and glossy volumes by celebrity chefs, all pictures and moody locations, stacked high on supermarket shelves. Then there are the telly programmes about regional food that dredge up long-gone delicacies – gulls' eggs anyone? And the vast number of reality television shows where the winning and losing is everything and the cooking merely a mechanic.

What, I wonder, do Brits really eat? What do people cook at home when there are no cameras about? Are there any good cooks in Britain? These questions would have remained dinner party chit-chat were it not for a series of troubling reports from the foodie frontline.

The Frozen Yorkshire

Everyone admires Delia Smith. Her classic book – *Delia Smith's Complete Cookery Course* – was first published in 1978 and has maintained its place on the short shelf of books I turn to most. Ms Smith stands for reliability, she's sensible, she's trustworthy. And then quite suddenly the roof fell in and there she is on television banging on about using frozen Yorkshire puddings and frozen ready-made mashed potato. Food is an intensely personal subject, but there are a handful of values most food writers and keen cooks share even if they don't always admit it. These are the big five: let's try and work with the seasons; let's eat fresh food; let's eat local food; let's try and eat more healthy food; let's only buy food as we need it. When judged by these criteria even contemplating a frozen Yorkshire pudding is bonkers. For a start making your own Yorkies is not rocket science. Yours will taste nicer. You won't have to go to three different supermarkets to assemble the ingredients for a meal. I haven't done the sums but I don't see how some flour, eggs and milk could be so costly as to make the frozen puds cheaper. The idea of using frozen mashed potato is even more chilling. Paying a premium to avoid peeling some spuds is perverse, and good mashed potato is such a joy. Delia, how could you? This whole business is like inviting an old family friend around for supper only for her to lean across the table and bite you.

The Potty-Mouthed Chef

I have eaten Gordon Ramsay's food on several occasions and I have had some excellent meals: interesting combinations of taste and texture, precise flavours, elegant dishes. But somewhere along the line the train has left the rails. Searching for better viewing figures is one thing but is a foul-mouthed boorish persona the best way to trap the ratings? It's an unpleasant truth but the Continentals are laughing at us – which wouldn't matter in itself if they hadn't spent the last twenty years chuckling as they dismissed British food and British cooks as of no account. If you search for 'T.V. Kantine – Gordon Ramsay' on youtube.nl you'll find a couple of minutes of video. It opens on a kitchen and the Gordon character swears and spits out various things he is given to taste. At the end of the clip one of the top chefs in the Netherlands, clad in immaculate whites and with a traditional tall white hat, enters stage left and pours a terrine of soup over 'Gordon's' head and walks off. The Dutch chef says nothing, he doesn't have to. How can it be that one of Britain's most fêted chefs is now only associated with potty-mouthed diatribes? How can it be that the demands of television have turned a stellar talent into a dubious caricature?

The Case of the Airline Sandwich

I flew to Jerez with a small party of other food writers to soak up all the sights, sounds and sherry of the famous Feria – an astonishing spectacle, partly horse show, partly week-long binge. We wandered through the cool bodega of Gonzalez Byass and had a splendid time. But not before several of our party had tried the chicken and bacon sandwich served from the trolley on the plane. I am aware that this particular sandwich has already enjoyed several column inches but I make no apologies for popping it back into the limelight. This sandwich represents everything that can go wrong with a food item. Let me share the pack copy. The selling bit read, 'Chicken breast blended with seasoned free range mayonnaise and rasher of smoke flavour sweetcure bacon and crisp lettuce on malted brown bread'. So far so good, and we would have munched away without a care had we not been food-obsessed on the one hand and bored by air travel on the other.

Here is the ingredients panel, and I assure you that this is not a joke. *Malted brown bread (52%) (wheat flour, water, malted wheat flakes, muscovado sugar, wheat gluten, barley malt flour, wheat bran, yeast, salt, spirit vinegar, emulsifiers E472(e), E481, E471, vegetable oil, flour treatment agent E300); chicken mayonnaise mix (27%) chicken breast (14%) (chicken breast, water, glucose syrup, thickener E1442 (from tapioca) salt, salt compound (sodium chloride, sodium citrate, sodium bicarbonate; free range mayonnaise (rapeseed oil, water, sugar, thickener E1422 (from maize), free range pasteurised egg yolk powder (free range pasteurised egg yolk, salt, maltodextrin), acidity regulator E260, salt, stabiliser E415, preservative E202, thickener E1422 (from maize), black pepper); smoke flavour sweetcure bacon (11%) pork belly, water, salt, porcine plasma, sugar, glucose syrup, thickener (potato starch), natural smoke flavour (stabilisers: E451, antioxidant E316, preservative E250), lettuce (8%), low fat spread (2%) (water, inulin, whey powder (from milk), milk protein, vegetable oil, thickener: potato starch, emulsifier E471, stabilisers E415, E471, salt, preservative E202, flavouring colour E1600a).*

So there you have it, the small print. All 150 words of it. Eighteen mentions of E numbers; 'free range mayonnaise' – presumably the jars can come and go as they please; a chicken breast that contains six ingredients; 'porcine plasma' – thank you Doctor; natural smoke flavour. Perhaps there is something to be said for what seem to be oppressive labelling regulations after all? For the record, that sandwich tasted very much as you would expect: soggy, sweet, salty. Why do we all put up with such things?

Just Over the Horizon

When food companies, restaurant entrepreneurs, drinks marketeers and the rest of the slick-suited gang hit a brick wall in their mission to think up something new for the British market, they book their best men a business class seat and send them to America. It is said that whatever is 'big' over there will be big over here in a year or two and in these credit crunch times that means fine-tuning an obsession with hamburgers and other fast food missions. Here are a couple of gleanings from the American viewpoint.

Todd Wilbur is something of a celebrity and is described as a 'best-selling cookbook author'. Each of his eight (a ninth is due to be published soon) books tells the reader how to recreate branded dishes at home. He has successfully 'cloned' the McDonald's Big Mac and a version of the Snickers candy bar; his latest triumph is to enable home cooks to make their own Kentucky Fried Chicken's Grilled

Chicken. In pursuit of the perfect recipe Wilbur 'uses a variety of techniques, including interviewing KFC employees at the drive-thru and analyzing an acquired sample of the secret seasoning'. You have to admire his tenacity; you have to admire the publishing industry for managing to make a success of the books; but you have to wonder if this is the future.

Elsewhere in the wonderful world of American food on the internet comes this awesome recipe – and while we cannot help wondering if it's a spoof, it sounds real enough to chill the blood.

Ingredients, to feed two
2 x 8oz barbecue burgers
4 strips of fried bacon
2 fried eggs
4 Krispy Kreme Donuts

METHOD
Place a donut on a plate, top it with a burger, then an egg, and then two strips of bacon. Then top the assembly with the second donut. 'The contrast between sweet and savoury is just unbelievable and downright delish!'

What on earth is going on? Is this the path that we in Britain are lurching towards?

Eat Up!
Against this ominous backdrop of mixed signals I decided to find out for myself just what was going on. I resolved to do some travelling and see just what state British cooking was in. My plan was to tour the country having meals with strangers and this book is the result. I have enjoyed the hospitality of ordinary, honest, capable cooks who have never sought the limelight. It's been a great deal of fun and extremely informative; each meal gets its own chapter and each chapter sets out the recipes. On my travels I also came across some unsung folk,

who despite having made an enormous contribution to Britain's food and drink culture don't seem to get the credit or media coverage they deserve. There are six of them and they also get a chapter each. (Why is it that all the food books cover the same ground over and over again? The same elver fisherman has been featured on numerous television programmes and in countless articles, even though we all know that eating elvers is now wholly irresponsible.)

So now I had a plan, to eat with strangers. But every plan comes with its own problems and the first was how to pinpoint people to dine with. I wanted confident people who enjoyed cooking and had some interesting recipes. I also wanted to find people who were not already famous or a part of the ever-expanding 'food media'. As is so often the case this kind of search is best handled by friends.

To find the cooks who people these pages I have bullied my friends mercilessly – and I owe them all a supersize thank you – they have called their friends and in some cases their friends have carried my proposition to an ever-widening circle. The profusion of good cooks out there is very encouraging – typically anyone I explained my rather eccentric plan to gave it a moment's thought and then came up with some names. As we can all name a few good cooks in our circle of acquaintance it seems likely that British cooking is alive and well but hiding.

The next problem is how to organise an extensive programme of eating – and one where I get to visit Aberdeen, Llanidloes, Newcastle, Wincanton and a host of places in between. In a less hurried, more prosperous, gentler, sort of world I would have set off (perhaps in a vintage open-topped sports car if the television producers took an interest) on a lengthy and glorious road trip. You know the kind of thing: 'And so we leave the bosky dells of Herefordshire and point the bonnet towards the metropolis of Birmingham.' The trouble is, life is no longer like that in this credit crunch age and I have a day job. The result is that I have had to eat these meals as and when it was expedient but they were no less enjoyable for that.

I still like the idea of one long journey of discovery. I also nurture a longing to star in a road movie, so I have arranged the chapters of this book as if they were a series of stops along one winding journey pausing to enjoy meals and also to visit the 'six of the best' unsung heroes. Thus we start in Brighton and end up in Grampound, Cornwall. Humour me, and let's pretend that I set out on a journey in search of good cooking in Britain and that now, several hundred miles later, I can report that I have found it in abundance.

LUNCH WITH
ROSIE AND ANDREW GIFFORD
HOVE, SUSSEX

BRIGHTON AND HOVE (both parts of the city demand equal billing) must be a pleasant place to live. It used to be a blowsy, elderly floozy of a seaside town, where the domes and minarets of the Brighton Pavilion seemed to merge right in. But with the elevation to City status things seem to have got a tad more refined: where once the eye was taken by students relieving themselves in doorways now there are film festivals, ambitious restaurants and gentle *Guardian*-reading intellectuals.

All of which makes it a well nigh perfect home for Rosie and Andrew Gifford. 'Giff' and Rosie enjoy swimming against the tide. While everyone else in Brighton would give their eyeteeth to live in the south-west of France, in 2007 the Giffords and their two children decided to move their base from a large house near Perigourd where they had lived for seven years to a smaller one in Hove. They still spend the summer in France but now their eight-year-old son Dylan plays his football with Brighton and Hove. This enviable lifestyle is underwritten by Giff's day job: he is a painter and his landscapes are much in demand, his shows at a West End gallery usually sell out and now he has his own studio in Brighton as well as the one at his other home in France. He wasn't always so prosperous or so famous. One evening a decade or so ago when travelling back on the underground after finishing a painting on Clapham Common he offered to sell it to his fellow tube travellers for £200 (even then his pictures fetched thousands rather than hundreds). There were no takers. What gives the story charm, however, is that some years later someone who had bought a picture at his private view confessed that he had been on the tube that night and had always regretted lacking the courage to speak up and buy the painting.

Rosie is by inclination a writer and home-maker and does most of the shopping and cooking for the family. But Giff reserves the right to interfere and will cook a dish every now and then. Living in France has given them both an insight into the relative state of the food culture on opposing sides of the Channel. As Rosie puts it, 'Food shopping in France can be limited, there is no chance of finding anything international in France, everything in France is French. When you look at the international ingredients section of French supermarkets there is just HP sauce and a lonely Edam cheese; in a decent UK supermarket you can buy the best ingredients from all over the world.' Because they have two children (bear in mind Lily is only two) and because their friends are in a similar position, the Giffords' social life revolves around having people round for dinner. 'A babysitter and taxis can cost as much as £50, which is a powerful incentive to stay at home and entertain.'

Despite their appreciation of British food and cooking, a little bit of Frenchness has rubbed off. Giff is manic about mushrooms and will wax eloquent about the relative merits of various rare edible mushrooms and while there are few ceps to be had in Brighton he has found mousserons – the 'fairy ring' mushrooms – on the football pitches where Dylan goes training. To get our lunch off to a good start Rosie opened with hot buttered oysters, a deft and simple combination of oysters cooked with garlicky butter. Then on to Giff's mushroom soup. He's obviously thought carefully about just what kind of soup best captures the real taste of wild mushrooms. His mushroom soup recipe is interesting because in a world that leans towards thick creamy soups he believes that you get better taste from thinner soup. For main course Rosie made one of those dishes that looks straightforward but calls for precision: scallops, prawns, quail's eggs, smoked cod, capers and a white sauce, all topped with fluffy potato. This was a fish pie on steroids. Pudding relied on the mulberry tree in the garden, that magnificent but rare soft fruit – so juicy, so sweet, so delicate. By way of a supporting cast for the mulberries there was a very rich flourless chocolate cake. Good cooking and plenty of original combinations of taste and texture.

HOT BUTTERED OYSTERS

Most cooks are a little bit in awe of oysters. They're pricey, they're difficult to open and there's always the worry that you may be handing out an unpleasant dose of food poisoning. Perhaps because they lived in France for seven years the Giffords are pretty relaxed about oysters. 'Cooking' them in this fashion (and with the flavour of garlic butter working its magic) makes them much more accessible, even to people who are not oyster lovers. Two per person makes a good pre-starter.

Serves 4

8 oysters	2 garlic cloves, finely crushed
50g unsalted butter	freshly ground black pepper

METHOD

1. Preheat the oven to 200°C/400°F/gas mark 6. You must start with live oysters – they are the ones that are holding their shells tightly closed. Discard any that are open. Open the oysters and cut them from the shell. Pop them into the bowl-shaped half shell.
2. Add a blob of butter, a little finely crushed garlic and a twist of freshly ground black pepper. Arrange the shells on a tray and bake for 7 minutes.

GIFF'S THIN MUSHROOM SOUP

Andrew Gifford (aka Giff) is mushroom mad. He picks and dries many kinds of wild mushroom and over the years his obsession has led him to experiment in his search for the 'best-ever' mushroom soup. It differs from most mushroom soups in that is not thick, chunky or creamy. Giff's soup is more like a consommé; it is not clear but it does carry a sledgehammer of flavour. He also recommends making it the day after you have had a roast chicken (or better still a roast duck): that way you can make a good stock. Supermarket chicken stock will do very nearly as well.

Serves 4

For the stock	*For the soup*
1 onion, peeled and finely chopped	1 onion, peeled and finely diced
1 leek, finely chopped	2 carrots, peeled and finely diced
2 carrots, peeled and finely chopped	1 potato, finely diced
20ml olive oil	25g unsalted butter
1 chicken or duck carcass, broken up	1 garlic clove, finely crushed
a few peppercorns	100g dried wild mushrooms – ceps, trom-
bouquet garni (rosemary, sage, bay leaf and	pettes de morts, winter chanterelles
stick of celery loosely tied together)	(the mixed forest mushrooms you can buy
175ml white wine	in packets will do fine)
	300g portobello mushrooms, finely diced
	30ml cognac
	bunch of flat-leaf parsley, finely chopped
	50ml single cream (optional)

METHOD

1. First make the stock. Fry the onion, leek and carrot in the oil until beginning to colour. Transfer to a stockpot with the carcass, peppercorns, bouquet garni and wine, then add water until everything is covered by 2cm. Bring to the boil slowly, then simmer gently for 3 hours. Strain and reduce until you have about 1.5 litres.

2. To make the soup, sweat the onions, carrot and potato in half the butter until soft. Add the garlic and cook for a further two minutes, then set aside.

3. Add the dried mushrooms to the stock, bring to the boil then turn off the heat and leave to infuse for 45 minutes. All the flavour will leach out of the mushrooms into the stock.

4. Sweat the portobello mushrooms in the remaining butter. Cook until the juices run.

5. Strain the soup and discard the wild mushrooms. Add the cooked portobello mushrooms and their juice along with the onion mixture. Bring to the boil and simmer for 20 minutes.

6. Strain the soup, pushing about an eighth of the vegetables through the sieve with a spoon. Add the cognac and chopped parsley. Serve, with a splash of cream if desired.

SCALLOP, PRAWN AND QUAIL'S EGG PARMENTIER

This is really a layered fish pie, but a very Ritzy one indeed. An implausibly short cooking time means you must only include fish and shellfish that can be eaten raw, such as large, cooked prawns.

Serves 4

400g smoked cod
1 litre whole milk
750g floury potatoes
150g large, cooked prawns
(frozen will be fine)
1 dozen quail's eggs, hardboiled and peeled
100g small button mushrooms,
halved

as many large scallops (without their corals)
as your wallet allows
2 tablespoons capers
freshly ground black pepper
50g butter
50g flour
salt
freshly ground nutmeg

METHOD

1. Preheat the oven to 180°C/350°F/gas mark 4. Poach the cod in the milk for about 5 minutes, then remove the fish and reserve the milk. Skin the cod and cut it into large pieces (about 6x3cm), you don't want it falling apart.
2. Boil the potatoes in salted water and mash – this is a rich dish so plain mash works best. Set aside.
3. Take a large, shallow ovenproof dish and arrange the prawns in the base. Add a layer of quail's eggs and mushrooms, followed by a layer of scallops and the fish pieces. Sprinkle with capers and season with pepper.
4. To make the white sauce, melt the butter in a pan, then stir in the flour. Reheat the milk in which you poached the cod and work this into the flour mixture a little at a time, stirring as you go until smooth. Season with salt and pepper and add nutmeg to taste.
5. Pour the sauce over the fish. Set aside for 5 minutes to allow a 'skin' to form, then cover with the mashed potato. Bake for 10–15 minutes, before browning under the grill.

ALMOND AND CHOCOLATE SLICE WITH MULBERRIES

This recipe is the direct descendent of various French and Italian 'flourless' chocolate cakes. It is very good indeed and the rich chocolate works amazingly well with the juicy sweetness of the fresh mulberries. You could substitute raspberries but they will only ever be an understudy to the magnificent mulberry.

Serves 4

125g dark chocolate, minimum 70% cocoa solids
1 tablespoon cognac
1 teaspoon vanilla extract
1 tablespoon strong black coffee
80g unsalted butter

80g caster sugar
80g very finely ground almonds
3 eggs, separated
250g mulberries
single or double cream, to serve (optional)

METHOD

1. Preheat the oven to 150°C/300°F/gas mark 2, and line a 20cm diameter sponge tin with baking parchment.
2. Melt the chocolate in a bowl set over boiling water (do not allow the bowl to touch the water). Add the cognac, vanilla extract and coffee, and stir in gently. Add the butter, sugar and ground almonds, stirring to mix well, then work the egg yolks into the mixture.
3. In a separate bowl, whisk the egg whites to stiff peaks. Fold the chocolate mixture and egg whites together, being careful to mix them well but keep things fluffy.
4. Pour the mixture into the tin and bake for about 45 minutes. Allow to cool.
5. Serve with a pile of mulberries on each slice and a spoonful of cream if desired.

THE WILD MAN

CANTERBURY, KENT

BY ANY OF THE NORMAL MEASURES Fergus Drennan is a pretty odd fellow. He is single-minded to the point of obsession and shockingly knowledgeable about all aspects of foraging. For Fergus, foraging is not some recently espoused, new age, eco-enthusiasm: he clearly remembers being fascinated by wild food even as a child. In the same way that you would bet upon a five-year-old Einstein's first doodles being equations, it seems likely that an infant Fergus would have been gurgling with pleasure when fed breast milk but appalled and screaming when offered a bottle of formula. This is a man who gets excited when talking about chipolatas made from road-kill badger; who is prepared to spend a day making flour from rosehip seeds; and who waxes lyrical about the flavours a few thousand sand hoppers can add to a bowl of soup.

On the last occasion that I met Fergus he was bubbling over with the fascinations of his latest projects (and it seems a dead cert that whenever you meet Fergus, while the projects will certainly be different, the enthusiasm will always be fever pitch). Wild garlic curd was claiming the greater part of his attention. This is a labour-intensive delicacy and to make it you start by picking 12kg of wild garlic leaves: liquidise these with plenty of water and then boil them up, which will coagulate the proteins. With any luck you'll end up with 800g of bright viridian green, pungently garlicky curd. Fergus uses it to flavour home-made tagliatelle. He also spent a lengthy spell trying to replicate Dr Seuss's 'green eggs with ham' by sitting an egg yolk on an emerald green portion of wild garlic curd. But, true to his philosophy of making use of every last bit of whatever he forages, the fibrous mass left over at the end of the curd-making process gets turned into paper and cardboard. He likes the idea of preparing a jar of wild garlic pesto and then presenting it in a small green cardboard box that is also made from wild garlic.

The one aspect of foraging that we are all happy to overlook – given our rose-tinted standpoint – is the brutal amount of hard work. Not many people would embark on an investigation of sand hoppers, particularly as they are so small (each tiny creature is about 1.8mm long). While gathering seaweed at Joss Bay Fergus noted that the middle strand line (that's the area that's not so far up the beach that it is baked dry, nor so close to the waves that it's always wet), was home to several million sand hoppers. Shake handfuls of seaweed over a bucket of seawater and you can gather tens of thousands of these miniscule creatures. Then the challenge is to separate the sand hoppers from the grains of sand and tiny seaweed rafts that they are clinging to. Take the hoppers home and start by straining your catch through a pillowcase, then set up a large tarpaulin in the garden, tying the corners to trees until you have a 'bowl'. Then you're ready to swirl the hoppers in sea water until they leave the crud behind – it's rather like panning for gold. A few hours' hard work and you can end up with 1.5kg of hoppers. The good news is they taste like tiny, crunchy shrimps. Try deep-frying them or pop them into a simple seaweed soup – they will add a savoury taste to the broth.

In a modern age when we all demand instant gratification, foraging presents one obstacle after another. If anyone tells you that it's your way to 'nature's supermarket' or your own 'garden of Eden' you would be right to punch them on the nose. To begin with, we should all be harvesting wild food sustainably and with permission of the land owner. And then there's the question of food miles – not in this instance the cost to the planet in jet fuel that enables us to enjoy imported out-of-season asparagus, but the sheer distances you have to cover when foraging. Sure, it's possible to forage all the ingredients for a dinner party but Nature is not a convenience store and you may have to drive to four or five habitats several miles apart to find what you want. Interesting? Certainly. Saving the planet? Hardly. Nomadic tribes living off the land were nomadic of necessity, travelling great distances to secure what they needed.

Since wild food has become fashionable on the menus of leading London restaurants a growing number of people have set up businesses to supply foraged ingredients. In this respect Fergus is a poacher turned gamekeeper because he once foraged commercially before scaling back his activities and now he no longer works on behalf of restaurants. It's about time the Environment Agency developed a coherent policy on foraging: in Scotland there are Park Rangers who enforce a code of conduct and in the New Forest the local authorities have made an attempt to regulate mushroom picking, but foraging is still very much a grey area. The significant distinction is between individuals who gather for their own consumption and professionals that forage to sell on. Fergus views foraging as much more than a free meal, he is convinced that we should all be learning about plants and the way they fit into a regional ecology: 'For me the major problem in Britain is the lack of connection between people and their food,' he says. 'The biggest threat is not over-picking but rather habitat loss. If we were all better connected to our food we would fight harder to preserve the differing habitats from which it comes.'

The seashore is a key resource for Fergus – there are 600 different varieties of seaweed to be found around Britain and currently they tend to be unexploited.

When Fergus holds one of his foraging courses, half the day is spent on the beach. As well as the gastronomic stars like carrageen (which makes a fine setting agent for milk puddings), there are dulse and pepper dulse (these are truly sea vegetables), sea lettuce and all the different kelps. Rather surprisingly Fergus contends that 'I have never met anyone who didn't like eating seaweed.' Perhaps it helps that the first seaweed they get to try on his course is deep-fried – history doesn't relate how the 4 litres of good oil with a high smoke point fits in with the foraging ethos. He is particularly fond of deep-fried bladder wrack but counsels that the little bell-shaped receptacles at the end of each frond need lengthy cooking before they are crisp.

In the summer of 2009 Fergus unleashed his most ambitious project – he knows that success is in no way guaranteed because several earlier attempts ended in failure. Fergus Drennan aimed to survive for a whole year sustained only by wild and foraged food. The complex demands of a healthy balanced diet mean that a good deal of preparatory work is called for. So last autumn he gathered 120kg of sweet chestnuts, which dried and ground up will provide porridge each morning for 150 days. He also gathered 120kg of acorns – think acorn coffee and acorn flour. However, acorns are overloaded with tannin and not fit for consumption, unless of course you take the trouble to leach out all the poisons. To do this, simply crack the acorns and pop them in sacks in a fast-flowing stream and the water will carry off the problem tannins. For this attempt Fergus put his acorns in to a leach year ahead of time. There's a cunning method you can use to try this process at home on a more manageable scale: take a handful of cracked acorns and hang them in a net in your toilet cistern – every time you flush it will change the water and wash away those bitter tannins! From his experiments Fergus reports that acorn flour has one very interesting property: it stops pastry shrinking. Adding 10 per cent acorn flour to rosehip, or chestnut, or Alexander root, or arum lily tuber, or plantain seed flour (or any other flour the well-stocked forager might decide upon) means there is no need to chill your pastry cases before baking; you become immune from shrinking or cracking.

Should you have the temerity to query how one can make pastry without fat, Fergus will happily discourse on the merits of badgers. In some quarters Fergus is known as the 'road-kill chef' and he makes a very cogent case against the wastage involved in all that dead wildlife even if his figures sound rather extravagant. He estimates that 10 million birds, 20,000 foxes and 50,000 badgers get killed on our roads every year. He goes on to speculate that if you assume that two million of the birds and all 50,000 badgers are edible (and that you can feed six people off a badger) we are wasting 2,300,000 meals a year! It's an eccentric and gloriously naïve viewpoint, but the badgers are an integral part of the plan for his wild food year. It turns out that badgers are fat creatures (and Fergus's statistics mean that they are a good deal more stupid than foxes – more than twice as likely to get run over). Each badger has 1.5kg of back fat, which Fergus painstakingly removes and processes. It takes three consecutive renderings before it loses an undesirable, gamey, badgery aroma, but persevere and you are left with a pure white, neutral fat that is excellent for pastry-making. Fergus has also perfected a recipe for badger chipolatas made in natural skins – the badger chitterlings need multiple washing and for the filling some rusk (perhaps from chestnut flour bread?) is the key as it binds the sausage meat together.

One of the major challenges of the wild food project will be satisfying a craving that afflicts us all, that imperative wish for something really sweet. During the berry season or the wild apple season it's a simple matter of picking and eating but how about in the dark days of winter? Fergus has prepared by laying in stores of fruit leathers – apples and berries harvested during the seasonal glut then cooked down to concentrate the sugars and the flavours before being dried out so that it keeps. Another luxury natural sweetener is made in the spring: birch sap syrup. It's a pity that the syrup maple doesn't grow in Britain as you only need 80 litres of maple sap to make a litre of syrup, whereas when it comes to the birch the ratio is a whopping 120 litres of sap to a single litre of syrup. As well as squirreling away a reserve of birch syrup each spring Fergus makes apple syrup and various berry syrups during the autumn.

If you ask Fergus what are his favourite foraging aids he replies that he uses a knife and a basket, but most of his recipes and techniques seem heavily reliant on pillowcases. As he talks about foraging you also become aware that it is not a way of life you can play at, or dip in and out of at will. Spring means Alexander stems, wild garlic, Japanese knotweed, sea kale, mushrooms. Summer means wild cherries (very sweet but with balancing acidity), also a banquet of different seaweeds. Autumn means another flush of mushrooms, a crop of different nuts, plus sea buckthorn berries. Fergus is convinced that sea buckthorn berries could become the next great superfood – he makes a juice that contains plenty of malic acid, is slightly pink and viscous, almost oily. The prescription is one small shot of sea buckthorn juice every morning – a flavour jolt so intense that it makes you shudder as it goes about its business of setting you up for the day.

It's refreshing to meet someone who is a good cook, well informed when it comes to nutrition and biochemistry and scarily enthusiastic but who doesn't pine for rarer and rarer, stranger and stranger foreign delicacies. Fergus Drennan wants first to understand and appreciate the flora and fauna we have on our doorstep – so much of which we overlook in our modern day ignorance.

DINNER WITH

JAMES MONTGOMERY

VAUXHALL, SOUTH LONDON

JAMES MONTGOMERY lives in a flat over a betting shop on one of south
London's busiest roads and is one of the prime movers in a cooking club called the
Gentleman Gourmands of London, which sounds a good deal more pompous than
it is in practice. Every month or so this gang of twenty-somethings holds a dinner.
The format is straightforward but rigorous – as befits a group where the majority
are graduates. Each man selected (girlfriends attend the dinners but the cooking
is the preserve of the gentlemen) cooks one of five courses that go to make up a
themed menu. The assembled company votes on the dishes and whoever cooked
the winning course gets to set the theme for the next event.

Past themes range from the simple 'winter warmer' or 'best of British' – that one
inspired a shepherd's pie made in the shape of the British Isles – to some more
esoteric challenges like 'Drake's Passage'. For this each cook was tasked with
cooking a dish that originated in one of the ports where Sir Francis Drake made
landfall during his voyage around the world – members of the club go misty-
eyed when recalling the magnificent Mussaman lamb curry from Cape Town
that triumphed on the night. It is heartening that a group (albeit a pretty bright

group) of young men think that cooking is important enough to take seriously. These people do not eat out continually in elite restaurants, they do not pore over cookery books or tune in to afternoon television, but they have a healthy interest in cooking new dishes. Thankfully they also understand that simple is good.

When asked how he came by this love of food James is quick to credit his parents, both of whom were accomplished cooks, and when asked to name his favourite 'signature' dish James opts for scrambled eggs, a choice that he shares with iconic nineteenth-century chef Auguste Escoffier. Scrambled egg is one of the most deceptive dishes there is, done badly (think grubby cafés and flabby eggs congealed by a jet of superheated steam blurting from the spout of an espresso machine) it is hideous, but when done well – made with artery clogging amounts of butter and cream, fresh eggs with radiant yolks, and the texture runny but not too runny – scrambled eggs are ambrosial. You have to warm to anyone who claims something that is both as simple and as difficult for his signature dish.

It's partly a result of living in London but there is an all-embracing feel to James's cooking. He's a bit of a chilli head and grows his own hot peppers, he also waxes lyrical about the Ethiopian shop in nearby Brixton Market – there you can buy the deadly Scotch bonnet peppers by weight. When it comes to food shopping he makes informed choices, buying chicken from the halal shop for a number of very good reasons – halal chickens are older and so have more taste, plus they are also much cheaper than their supermarket cousins.

I didn't attend a meeting of the Gentleman Gourmands of London because I wanted to try a three course menu from James Montgomery, but there were several rather critical members of the club around the dinner table. James's menu started with a courgette soup. This dish was surprisingly sophisticated and had a very interesting texture – by using a grater to pare off long, thin strips of courgette the finished soup seemed to have body. The addition of a spoonful of chilli salsa to each bowl gave a welcome boost. James cooks well and has an agreeably unfussy attitude – he uses stock cubes, ready-made condiments and frozen peas.

When it came to the second course – a chicken, leek and bacon pie – the pastry was ready made from the supermarket. It put me in mind of the Michelin-starred chef Nico Ladenis, who shocked the purists when he acknowledged that even his flagship restaurant bought in bread rolls rather than making them from scratch. Nico justified his policy by saying that if bought-in bread was better quality than he could make in his kitchen, it was the sensible option. For his dessert James made what seemed like a traditional French chocolate mousse, but one that was given a novel twist by the use of Maya Gold, a spicy chocolate from Green & Black's. The bourbon and mint milkshake he served with the mousse was exceedingly delicious and as the saying goes 'probably deserves a show of its own'!

COURGETTE SOUP WITH ROAST TOMATO SALSA

James Montgomery has an implacable fondness for chilli, but in this dish he reins it in so that there is merely a hint of warmth within the salsa. On the face of it courgette soup sounds as if it might be a rather watery prospect but by grating them finely the courgettes end up adding texture – the long strips are much the same size and shape as vermicelli. Feel free to vary the proportions of solid to liquid if you like your soup thinner. The salsa is dolloped into each bowl of soup before serving to give the dish an intriguing chilli kick.

Serves 6

3 garlic cloves
1 teaspoon dried thyme leaves
1 teaspoon dried oregano
1 teaspoon ground coriander
2 large onions, finely sliced
1 dessertspoon olive oil
850ml vegetable stock (homemade or from a stock cube)
4 courgettes
salt and freshly ground black pepper

For the roast tomato salsa
4 large tomatoes, deseeded
1 red pepper
2 hot chillies, deseeded (if desired) and finely chopped
up to 1 tablespoon olive oil
up to 1 tablespoon balsamic vinegar
salt and freshly ground black pepper

METHOD

1. Preheat the oven to 220°C/425°F/gas mark 7. Peel the garlic cloves and parcel them up in foil with the thyme and oregano. Pop them in the oven until the garlic is soft – about 20 minutes. At the same time, roast the tomatoes and pepper for the salsa, also for about 20 minutes.
2. Meanwhile, sprinkle the coriander over the onions, and fry them in the olive oil until softened.
3. Put the softened garlic and the onions into a liquidiser or food-processor with a little of the vegetable stock and whiz until you have a purée.
4. Put the remaining vegetable stock into a large saucepan and add the onion and garlic purée.

5. Grate the courgettes – you are aiming for long, very thin, strips – about the size and shape of vermicelli – the kind of mandolin grater used for making celeriac remoulade is the perfect tool. Add to the pan and simmer on a low heat for about 20 minutes – do not boil the courgettes to mush!

6. To complete the salsa, remove the skins and chop the tomatoes and pepper (make the pepper pieces slightly smaller than the tomatoes). Place in a bowl with the chillies and use the olive oil and balsamic vinegar to adjust the consistency to taste and then season.

7. Check the seasoning of the soup and serve with a blob of salsa in the centre of each bowl.

CHICKEN, LEEK AND BACON PIE

A jolly good and jolly simple pie. James gets his chicken from a nearby halal shop as the birds are that bit older and tougher – they hold their shape better in the final pie. He also uses bacon chops – because they are thicker than rashers you can cut them into chunky lardons. The one somewhat unusual ingredient is a branded Japanese condiment – Nanami Togarashi – which is a seven-spice blend of different chillies with some dried orange peel, sesame seeds, seaweed and ginger. If this proves hard to find, ground mixed peppercorns, chilli flakes or even freshly ground black pepper would deliver a similar punch.

Serves 6

4 smoked bacon chops
3 leeks, finely sliced
3 large halal chicken fillets
2 chicken stock cubes
1 tablespoon plain flour
pinch of Nanami Togarashi

2 tablespoons mascarpone cheese
375g pack ready-made butter puff pastry
1 egg
salt and freshly ground black pepper

METHOD

1. Preheat the oven to 200°C/400°F/gas mark 6. Cut the bacon chops into chunky lardons and fry them in a dry pan until they release their fat. Add the leeks and cook until softened. Cut the chicken into chunks, roll in seasoned flour, then add to the bacon and leeks and cook until the chicken is browned and cooked through.
2. Make up the stock in a saucepan (using 20 per cent less water than instructed) and add a good shake of Nanami Togarashi. Mix the flour to a paste with a little water and add to the pan, stirring until thickened. Finally add the mascarpone.
3. Put the bacon, leeks and chicken into a large traditional pie dish with a wide rim and then pour over the stock mixture. Place a pie funnel in the middle to support the pastry.
4. Roll out your pastry and put a strip around the rim of the pie dish before topping the pie. Glaze with a little beaten egg. Bake for 30–40 minutes until the pastry is cooked and golden. Serve with green peas (frozen will do fine) and mashed potato enlivened with butter and either a hint of garlic or some horseradish.

MAYA GOLD MOUSSE SERVED WITH A BOURBON AND MINT MILKSHAKE

Maya Gold is a dark organic chocolate bar made by Green & Black's. It is dark and rich with a high percentage of cocoa solids and has subtle flavours of citrus and cinnamon. It is widely available in supermarkets but if it remains elusive use another good-quality dark chocolate.

Serves 6

6 large eggs
200g Maya Gold chocolate
225ml double cream

For the milkshake
leaves from a large bunch of fresh mint
1 small tub (100ml) good-quality
vanilla ice cream
6 shots of bourbon
milk

METHOD

1. Separate the egg yolks from their whites and put the whites into a scrupulously clean mixing bowl. Reserve the yolks.
2. Melt the chocolate in a bowl over a pan of boiling water (do not allow the bottom of the bowl to touch the water). Allow the chocolate to cool but not solidify and mix in the egg yolks – this is a tricky procedure, too hot and the eggs will curdle, too cool and the chocolate will be solid. You are aiming for the perfect mid-point compromise! Fold the cream into the chocolate mixture.
3. Whisk the egg whites to stiff peaks, then fold into the chocolate mixture. You are aiming to preserve the bubbles and lightness, so do not overwork the mixture. Use to fill six ramekins and chill until set, preferably overnight.
4. To make the milkshake, place the mint leaves, ice cream and bourbon in a liquidiser and whizz thoroughly. Add milk, a little at a time, whizzing to mix, until you have the degree of milkshake 'thickness' you prefer. Serve in small glasses with the mousse.

THE ROASTERS

ESSEX

I FIRST MET JEREMY TORZ AND STEVEN MACATONIA in 1995 when I ventured out to the wilds of Essex and a small, ramshackled, wooden building that they called the 'shed'. Inside was an elderly machine that had much in common with an early steam engine: lots of black, polished dials, levers, hot and hissing – this was their pride and joy, a small-batch coffee roasting machine. The fun got started when the roast began – two precise if eccentric men in spectacles danced around the machine tweaking a knob here and adjusting a lever there until the grand moment when the hot beans were swept out of the machine to cool. Until that point I had never considered that coffee roasting might make exciting spectator sport, or appreciated that timing was everything – 30 seconds too long in the flames could downgrade the coffee from perfection to ordinary. These guys were obsessive and it showed in their jaw-droppingly delicious coffee.

It's unlikely that career advisors in the 1980s were clued up on the potential of the coffee roasting business so it is no surprise that when they met Steven had acquired a PhD in cellular immunology and a promising career in research while Jeremy was an optician working in a contact lens practice. They were both feeling in need of a change so Jeremy resigned, Steven took a sabbatical and they both moved to northern California. It wasn't that difficult a decision. Britain was mired in a recession and they were relocating to somewhere that had just invented farmer's markets, enjoyed a year-long growing season and had a burgeoning food and restaurant culture. After considering opening a bakery and café (their trademark attention to detail meant that Steven enrolled at the Californian Culinary Academy's evening classes in chocolate work and patisserie, while Jeremy went to work for Peet's, the grand-daddy of American coffee shops) they gradually came to the conclusion that they were destined to work in the coffee business.

As Steven puts it, 'Coffee roasting allows you to put over your own style, it is an interpretive process. First take green coffee beans from a particular source and, then so much depends on how you roast them. You walk a tightrope between the beans and flames.' Before Alfred Peet opened for business in the 1960s American coffee was wishy-washy, limpid stuff fit only for cowboys. Peet roasted his coffee until it was several times darker than that of his contemporaries. The 'coffee revolution' started in Berkeley, California, and quickly spread to Seattle, mainly due to the intervention of 'life-changers' like Steven and Jeremy.

It seems that OCD (obsessive compulsive disorder) is a vital asset to an expert coffee roaster. Attention to the tiniest detail is of paramount importance, and fortunately this bizarre intensity comes naturally to Steven and Jeremy. They resolved to return home and set up a coffee business in London. As Jeremy puts it, 'People do recognise a better cup of coffee. They may not know what makes it better, but they do know when it is better.' In 1994 they slept in a tent (no money for hotel rooms) while attending a coffee conference in Vienna. They had persuaded the American manufacturers of a small-batch coffee roaster, to display the machine at the Conference but then to sell it to the newly formed Torz &

Macatonia, thus saving them the lion's share of the shipping charges. This is the machine that ended up in an Essex shed.

The next problem was to source green beans for roasting, and that proved to be more difficult than you would expect. The UK coffee dealers saw their business as commodity trading – quality considerations coming a very long way behind price. When asked to supply anything rare or special they were more puzzled than helpful. So for the very early years of their business the green coffee beans came via the USA. Today, in a world concerned about air miles and green issues, the memory of their coffee beans going round the world from Ethiopia to America to Britain still makes Jeremy and Steven sweat a bit. Then some German coffee dealers stepped into the breach and finally T&M started to import their own beans.

Pretty soon the shed in Essex was supplying bespoke blends and fine coffees to enlightened restaurants like the River Café and enlightened chefs like Raymond Blanc. Then, one afternoon, there was a breakthrough. While watching a foodie programme they caught sight of a coffee shop being used as the background to a shot – it was Britain's first Seattle Coffee Company outlet, and after checking where it was (by ringing the BBC duty desk) Jeremy rushed down to Covent Garden to try the coffee. Pretty soon all 60 branches of the Seattle Coffee Company were using T&M coffee and Steven and Jeremy were handling barista training and equipment set up. It was a case of stepping into the big time.

Not long afterwards, T&M merged with the Seattle Coffee Company and moved to a smart new roastery in Canning Town. Then in 1998 the American giant Starbucks engulfed the Seattle Coffee Company. Tactfully enough, Jeremy describes the 18 months they spent as part of the megacorp as 'an opportunity to work in a corporate environment, and see inside one of America's most successful businesses.' An outsider could have predicted that Jeremy and Steven would soon be off. They are more at ease with a company philosophy driven by a sense of difference than an unswerving regard for balance sheets. Inevitably the commercial juggernaut had eased them from being a coffee business to a business that does coffee. Furthermore the Starbucks ethos revolves around the North American palate, UK consumers may love the convenience of the US coffee shop model but they want it wrapped in European style and sophistication.

At about the time when Jeremy and Steven were saying farewell to Starbucks there was a spectacular collapse in the international coffee price, bringing tough times and poor prospects to many growers, particularly those in central America. It was also the beginning of the Fairtrade movement so perhaps there was a change in the prevailing mood. Jeremy and Steven set up Union Hand-Roasted, their third, and arguably most successful, coffee business. Jeremy explains, 'We're not entrepreneurs. We're not business people. For us it's all about the coffee, but until we set up Union we hadn't really got our boots dirty and got involved with the producers. The basis of Union was that all the many participants should be genuinely involved. We were looking for long-term relationships.'

This philosophy has meant a fair amount of globetrotting as it hinges on having a personal relationship with growers on the other side of the world. When the grower finally understands that the contract can be relied upon; that quality is important; and that the volume of coffee bought each year will remain stable and usually increase, it changes his mindset. A perfect example is the Santa Ana farm in Guatemala, where several years of being able to rely on Union rather than the vagaries of the commodity coffee market has meant that the plantation can expand and has been able to build new accommodation for its workers. Formerly the itinerant coffee pickers would stop off for a fortnight and then move on. The new, superior facilities mean that they now stay put for the season. Continuity and skill are crucial factors as the coffee bush will have ripe, over-ripe and under-ripe berries on the same branch at the same time. When we lean on the plunger to suppress the grounds in our shiny cafetière we are relying on the picker being conscientious, as the grading process starts with the picker.

A happy, skilful workforce at one end of the bush-to-cup continuum means a good brew at the other. As Jeremy says, 'For us coffee is personal, not marketing, and at

Santa Ana the coffee has got better, it definitely tastes cleaner. And that benefits everyone.'

If you ask Jeremy and Steven what qualities go towards the perfect cup of coffee, their spectacles glint as they interrupt one another continually – they just about agree that excellence is interlinked with acidity and balance. For decades the British coffee market has been dominated by millions of jars of instant coffee, and that has meant that pretty much whatever goes into one end of the factory will come out as brown granules the other. The knock-on effect of that commercial pressure has been higher and higher demand for cheaper and cheaper coffee. But quite suddenly Britons have woken up to the joys of a really good cup of coffee. This rare beast has a fruitiness and sweet clarity of flavour; it's never muddy, astringent or hard on the palate. A degree of acidity is the hallmark of elegant coffee. Jeremy tries to pin down this elusive quality: 'Balanced acidity is like the difference between a green apple and a crisp apple, one is more strident, the other more satisfying. There should also be a masked sweetness, the kind of flavours you find in a banana that is at the point of perfect ripeness.'

They are both a little bit coy about the strange over-the-top vocabulary that seems to be de rigueur when coffee tasting. Jeremy tells of being on a judging panel for the Cup of Excellence competition in Guatemala. Together with two dozen coffee experts from around the world he had sipped and slurped his way through hundreds of samples before one of the other judges said of the winner, 'This coffee was so clean and clear that it was like standing on top of a mountain. You can just see for miles.' Florid stuff, but you know what he means: good coffee is a subtle and rewarding multi-sensory experience. Jeremy is not immune from the perils of coffee-speak: he once described tasting a washed Harar coffee from eastern Ethiopia as a 'blueberry cheesecake' moment. Indignantly asserting that he could detect the fruit of the blueberries; the creaminess of the cheesecake; and the toasted flavours of the biscuit base.

What is charming about the Union Hand-Roasted business is the single-minded dedication of all its staff. This is an organisation that is focussed on coffee rather than profit, indeed it offers valuable and practical help to third world growers. Steven emphasises that 'It is always about the coffee – it has to be.' The British take on coffee culture is changing and as ever the boys have a simile that sums up their viewpoint. A good cup of coffee is like an Indian meal: ten years ago you went for the hottest curry on the menu, harsh and aggressive was the watchword – a vindaloo moment – but gradually we are all learning better and now we look for balanced spicing and subtlety in our Indian food and in our coffee.

'We are still doing what first brought us into the business,' says Jeremy, 'looking for the coffees we want to drink.'

'And currently the quality of green coffees on the world market is higher than ever before, and buyers are starting to respect the efforts of producers,' chips in Steven. These two really are obsessed with coffee. For the rest of us who enjoy specialist single estate coffees and elegant blends that is no bad thing.

LUNCH WITH
AMANDA WOODCRAFT AND FAMILY
MERSEA ISLAND, ESSEX

BEN WOODCRAFT is a fisherman turned fishmonger so it's no surprise that he wooed Amanda, his wife-to-be, with fish. On one notable occasion he turned up at her flat late at night with a spanking fresh sea trout so large that it had to be lopped in half before it would fit in the oven. This was all some time ago as they have lived on Mersea Island since 1998 and now have three children, Ned, thirteen, Paddy, ten, and Tess, six. Before moving to the cottage they lived on the much smaller Osea Island and before that Ben had the distinction of being the last fisherman to work out of the Heybridge Basin. Now he sells fish and deals with a roll call of chic London restaurants.

If the Woodcrafts were any more involved with the sea they would have webbed feet. Ben buys and sells fish, Amanda cooks fish and the whole family is sailing mad. The boys race dinghies each weekend and Ben can sometimes be found at the wheel of one of the large and elegant oyster smacks. Their clapboarded cottage is towards the east end of the island and it's no shock to see all shapes and sizes of children tucking into oysters as Amanda bustles around preparing lunch.

The fish we are to eat is sea bass. Ben has selected three 1kg fish for the party of five adults, 'They were caught two days ago by Gary. I would tell you where but even in these days of electronic fish finders the best fishing spots are still closely guarded secrets.' One of the unintended consequences of the mobile phone revolution is the way they have helped the fishermen. In the 1980s a fisherman could only contact shore or other boats via the VHF radio, so when telling a chum what you had caught and where you had caught it, you shared your secrets with anyone who had a radio set. Now Ben gets regular, and secure, telephone calls from the fishermen he works with and the fish they catch has often found a buyer before it even reaches port.

Fishing in Britain is in a terrible mess. The European Community imposed a quota system in a misguided attempt to regulate fishing. This system works well for shoal fish such as mackerel or sardines – when you net a shoal of mackerel that's pretty much what you get. Where the system collapses is when it is applied to other fish species (such as cod, whiting or haddock). Where these fish are concerned fishermen can shoot the nets aiming for whiting, a species for which they have 'quota' and end up with a catch that is mainly cod. Then, and this is the wicked wasteful bit, the fishermen are obliged to throw the dead cod back into the sea. The quota system also favours the bigger boats that fish on an industrial scale: 96 per cent of the British fish quota is 'owned' by 15 per cent of the fleet. Between 1988 and 2008 Britain lost half its fishing fleet, so whoever the Common Fisheries Policy may be helping, it certainly isn't the British fisherman or the British cook. If you would like to know more about these irrational and unsuccessful attempts to regulate our fishing industry take a look at the NUTFA site on the internet. This oddly named organisation (New Under Ten Fishermens' Association) has been set up to represent the interests of all those fishermen whose boats are under ten metres in length – these are the 85 per cent of fishing vessels that must make do with 4 per cent of the quota and throw back perfectly edible fish.

On a sunny spring day Mersea Island is at once an idyllic and curiously old-fashioned place. While the children play in the garden Amanda cooks lunch in the kitchen with her friend Sarah Cherry, who makes some delicious anchovy, parmesan and chilli biscuits. Amanda's menu is gloriously simple and under-pinned by fresh fish and asparagus from the garden. We start with a large bowl of home-made potted shrimps with good bread; then the sea bass, roasted and served with a dish of new potatoes and asparagus, on the side a 'green sauce' that delivers the tang of capers and a sweetish hint of mint. Finally, rhubarb and custard creams – which a posh restaurant would certainly call crème brûlée. Dishes are considered and elegant in their simplicity, seasoning spot on and flavours and textures neatly balanced. You don't have to be married to a fishmonger to enjoy food like this, but it helps! One thing we can all do to support real fishmongers and hard-pressed fishermen is eat more fresh fish and that is more of a pleasure than a duty.

SARAH CHERRY'S ANCHOVY, PARMESAN AND CHILLI BISCUITS

These biscuits make a fine nibble with pre-lunch drinks. They are simple to make and when they're baking will fill your kitchen with a most appetising smell. The uncooked dough can also be frozen for use at a later date – allow to thaw before slicing. If you don't like chillies leave them out, but they add another dimension to these crispy crunchy 'amuse-bouches'.

Serves 6

1 tin of anchovies in oil, drained
110g unsalted butter
110g parmesan, finely grated

110g plain flour
2 hot fresh red chillies, deseeded and
finely chopped

METHOD

1. Preheat the oven to 220°C/425°F/gas mark 7. Place all the ingredients in a food-processor and whizz until you have a crumbly biscuit dough.
2. Roll the dough into a log and wrap it tightly in greaseproof paper or baking parchment. Chill in the fridge for at least 1 hour before use.
3. To cook simply cut the log into slices about the thickness of a £1 coin and bake the biscuits on a parchment-lined tray. They should take 10–12 minutes, but much depends on how thinly you slice them. Watch carefully and remove them when they are golden brown. Eat warm from the oven.

POTTED SHRIMP

Having a fisherman and fishmonger for a husband obviously helps, but placing a large willow pattern bowl of potted shrimps in the middle of the table and handing round some fresh bread is a sure-fire way to impress. Because they have a higher iodine content than their larger cousins the prawns, the tiny brown shrimps also deliver more flavour and an uncanny sweetness, so when 'potting' you can team them with strong flavours.

Serves 6

1 shallot, peeled and finely diced	150g unsalted butter, cubed
2 tablespoons Manzanilla sherry	juice of 1 lemon
1 teaspoon cayenne pepper	400g peeled brown shrimps
3 blades of mace, broken into shards	salt and freshly ground black pepper
1 bay leaf	

METHOD

1. Put the shallots, sherry, cayenne, mace and bay leaf into a saucepan. Stir as it comes to the boil. Reduce until the liquid has almost vanished; the shallot pieces should be merely glistening.
2. Remove from the heat and add the butter. Return to a low heat until the butter has melted. You want the flavours to infuse the butter, so leave it on the lowest possible heat for 15 minutes or so, stirring from time to time. Remove from the heat and leave in a warm place to cool gently for about 30 minutes.
3. When the butter is cool but not set, pass the mixture through a fine sieve, pressing out all the flavour from the shallots. Combine the flavoured butter with the lemon juice, mix in the shrimps and season to taste with salt and pepper. You can pot the mixture in individual pots but it looks better in a large bowl. Be careful not pack everything too tightly; you need to strike a balance between coating the shrimps evenly and leaving them intact.
4. Cover and chill for at least three hours. Remove from the fridge and allow to rest at room temperature for 30 minutes before serving.

ROAST SEA BASS WITH GREEN SAUCE

'First catch your fish!' Or, for most of us, enlist the help of your fishmonger. You will need one sea bass between two people, always presuming that the fish are the perfect size for eating (between 1kg and 1.5kg). The smaller 'one-portion' farmed sea bass – many of which come from the Gironde estuary in France – are very much a second-best option as they do not have the firm texture of a freshly caught wild fish. Amanda's approach to this dish is very straightforward: she makes the green sauce, then roasts asparagus before jumbling it up with boiled new potatoes and serving it in a large platter on a bed of rocket. Then everything waits, pleasantly lukewarm, while she concentrates on the fish.

Serves 6

6 sea bass fillets, from three 1kg fish
(see above)

For the green sauce
1 garlic clove , peeled
6 anchovy fillets, drained
small jar of capers, drained
1 tablespoon Dijon mustard

1 tablespoon lemon juice
a large handful of fresh parsley
other herbs, e.g. tarragon, mint, basil
(you choose which and the proportions,
the parsley should dominate, the mint
adds a fresh note)
250ml extra virgin olive oil
salt and freshly ground black pepper

METHOD

1. First make the green sauce. Whizz the garlic, anchovies, capers, mustard and lemon juice with a hand-held blender or food processor until they come together as a gloopy liquid.

2. Chop the green herbs on a board. Don't overdo it, it is better that some texture remains. Mix together the garlic mixture, olive oil and herbs. Season to taste and serve in a bowl to accompany the fish.

3. For the sea bass, preheat the oven to 180°C/350°F/gas mark 4. Oil the fillets, sprinkle with lemon juice and season with salt and pepper. Roast them skin side up (you are aiming for a crisp skin) for about 10 minutes – watch it carefully, it is cooked when nicely firmed up.

RHUBARB AND CUSTARD CREAMS

These puds may sound as if they belong in a 1950s sweetshop but they are an altogether more sophisticated take on a classic flavour combination. The top part has the yielding texture of a good crème brûlée – which is pretty much what it is – but 'custard' has definite menu appeal.

Serves 6

400g rhubarb	1 vanilla pod
25g light demerara sugar	6 egg yolks
600ml single cream	50g golden caster sugar

METHOD

1. Preheat the oven to 150°C/300°F/gas mark 2. Take six ramekins. Chop the rhubarb finely and divide between them, sprinkling a little demerara sugar onto each. Bake for 10–15 minutes until the rhubarb is softened.
2. To make the topping, pour the cream into a pan. Split the vanilla pod and strip the seeds into the cream, adding the pod as well. Bring to the boil, then turn off the heat and allow to infuse as it cools for about 20 minutes.
3. Beat the egg yolks and the caster sugar together. Add the cream (removing the vanilla pod) and mix thoroughly. Pour the cream mixture over the rhubarb in the ramekins. Place the ramekins in a roasting tin filled to about 2cm with water and bake for about 8–10 minutes – they should be barely set.
4. Serve at room temperature (if you have kept them in the fridge allow them to warm up). The pecan biscuits will add a welcome crunch.

PECAN BISCUITS

These sweet biscuits have a welcome crunch that is the perfect foil to the rhubarb and custard creams (see previous recipe). As with the Anchovy, Parmesan and Chilli Biscuits, the uncooked dough log can be frozen for use at a later date.

Serves 6

50g pecan nuts	75g light brown sugar
125g unsalted butter	1 egg
200g plain flour	

METHOD

1. Preheat the oven to 150°C/300°F/gas mark 2. Take six ramekins. Chop the rhubarb finely and divide between them, sprinkling a little demerara sugar onto each. Bake for 10–15 minutes until the rhubarb is softened.
2. Put the pecans, butter, flour, sugar and egg into in a food processor and whizz until you have a crumbly biscuit dough. Roll the dough into a log and wrap it tightly in greaseproof paper or baking parchment. Chill in the fridge for at least 1 hour before use.
3. To cook, simply cut the log into slices about the thickness of a £1 coin and bake the biscuits on a parchment-lined tray. They should take about 15 minutes, but much depends on how thinly you slice them. Watch carefully and remove them when they are golden brown.

LUNCH WITH
CLARE HUGHES
WEST BRIDGFORD, NOTTINGHAM

UNSEASONAL SUNLIGHT streamed into the elegant green painted conservatory tacked onto the back of a spacious Edwardian house. The conservatory acts as a dining room for the Hughes family and segues into a state-of-the-art kitchen, a real cook's kitchen with a range cooker and plenty of cherished pots, pans and knives. It's Clare's kitchen. Clare Hughes started out as a primary teacher but has subsequently switched careers to become a researcher for television companies. She lives in West Bridgford with her husband John – a television sound man – and her young son Will. None of this information prepared me for the lunch that was to come. Clare is a very accomplished and precise cook and the dishes she most enjoys cooking are Spanish.

The lunch started with a few tapas and splendid crusty bread – Catalan spinach, sloppy, creamy and beguilingly rich; small squares of crisp roast pork belly; a dish of morcilla and apples; and a splendid tortilla, soggy and savoury. Then the main course: pollo al ajillo with white beans – the best kind of rich chicken stew, served with roast carrots and a dish of purple sprouting with pine nuts and raisins. Pudding was a sharp lemon cream served with chewy Amaretto macaroons.

Just reading the menu provokes a list of questions. Why this love of Spanish food? Where do you get morcilla (the soft and savoury Spanish variant on black pudding) in Nottingham? And where do such authentic and challenging recipes come from? If you're expecting to hear about a Spanish branch of the family, or several years spent living in Spain you'll be disappointed. Clare's passion for all things Spanish stems from a succession of Spanish holidays, but unlike most tourists Clare has taken a night school course to learn Spanish, and she discusses the variations in Spanish regional cuisine with knowledge and irrepressible enthusiasm. The old adage is true, to be a good cook one must first be good at eating.

Clare's mum was a trained pastry chef but, as Clare points out, in the 1950s the role of pastry chef was nowhere near as highly regarded as it is today and they spent long hours baking for modest returns. 'The one invaluable thing my mother taught me was to be organised in the kitchen.' Clare's dad was a chemist and she describes him as an 'experimental cook'. During the 1960s his job took him, and the whole family, to Singapore for $2^1/2$ years. Somewhere along the line Clare picked up a love of intense flavours and bold cooking that is tempered by a grasp of the importance of technique.

As you'd expect from someone so entranced by Spanish food you'll find all the Moro cookbooks on a shelf in the kitchen, but there are also books by Nigel Slater, Anjum Anand and Madhur Jaffrey. The problem of finding authentic Spanish ingredients is also easily resolved – should you live in Nottingham. Clare's local delicatessen stocks an impressive range up to, and including, morcilla.

It may be that Britons are uniquely qualified to bring out the best in foreign cuisines. Chefs born and bred in Britain head up several of London's Michelin-starred Italian, Spanish and French restaurants and there must be more to it than simply mastering continental techniques. When bitten by the cooking bug Brits have a remarkable lack of prejudice – cooks from France hold their own cuisine in such esteem that they rarely consider turning their hand to British or Spanish dishes. But with our open-mindedness comes a vital willingness to experiment.

Clare's dishes may have a recognisably Spanish heritage but they are also very accessible and the recipes have a practicality about them. Keeping a tin of ghee in the refrigerator for those occasions when you need clarified butter is one of the sensible shortcuts I always mean to get around to. If it's not too glib a summation, Clare's cooking is a mixture of passion and pragmatism with a distinctive Spanish accent.

MARINATED BELLY PORK

Clare served the belly pork cut into little squares – the perfect tapas, mouthfuls of seasoned crispness. Bully your butcher into cutting you a nice piece of lean pork belly.

Serves 4

1kg of belly pork, deboned

For the marinade
3 garlic cloves, peeled
salt and freshly ground black pepper

2 tablespoons fennel seeds
juice and zest of 1 lemon
2 tablespoons olive oil
splash of white wine vinegar

METHOD

1. The marinade is best made in a pestle and mortar, but if you don't have one use a big bowl and crush everything separately. Take your mortar and cream the peeled garlic cloves with a couple of pinches of salt. Add the fennel seeds and crush, then add the lemon juice, zest and olive oil and mix well.
2. Apply the mix to the meaty side of the pork, leaving the skin side dry to ensure good crackling. Let the pork rest in the fridge for up to 4 hours.
3. Preheat the oven to 220°C/425°F/gas mark 7. Wipe the pork skin with vinegar and season with salt. Put it into the top of the oven for 30–45 minutes until the skin blisters and crackles. Turn the oven down to 160°C/325°F/gas mark 3 and cook for a further 90 minutes. Remove the meat from the oven and rest for at least 30 minutes. Serve warm, cut into small squares.

TORTILLA

Clare makes a delicious tortilla and she puts her success down to two things – a favourite deep (4cm) but small diameter (20cm) iron frying pan, and practice. As she says, 'You just have to feel your way by trial and error'.

Serves 6

25ml olive oil	6 eggs
1 large sweet Spanish onion, finely sliced	salt and freshly ground black pepper
200g waxy potatoes, very finely sliced	

METHOD

1. Heat half the oil, add the onion and cook until soft but not browned. Set aside. Heat the remaining oil and cook the potatoes until soft and translucent.
2. Beat the eggs in a large bowl and season well. Stir in the onions and potatoes, mix thoroughly and transfer back to your frying pan. Cook gently on the hob for 15–20 minutes, and then finish under the grill. This is where the trial and error comes in: the best advice is to keep testing the tortilla with a skewer until it is soft all the way through. Serve warm.

MORCILLA WITH APPLE

Rather than olive oil Clare uses ghee for this classic fried dish – it's a good move as ghee is readily available in tins at ethnic shops and saves you the bother of clarifying butter. The higher cooking temperature achieved means that the apples caramelise well. If you cannot get morcilla – the Spanish black sausage – black pudding will be fine.

Serves 4

1 tablespoon ghee	250g morcilla
2 Cox's apples, cored and cut into wedges (do not peel)	salt and freshly ground black pepper

METHOD

Heat the ghee, add the apples and cook until golden brown. Add the morcilla and cook gently until hot through (morcilla can be very soft and crumbly, British black pudding is more robust). Season to taste.

CATALAN SPINACH

A dish that has its origins in a family-run Spanish hotel called Can Boix in Peramola, Catalonia, this is the latest recipe in a series of attempts by Clare to recreate the dish she remembers – she reckons it is getting pretty close!

Serves 4

10ml olive oil
1/2 sweet Spanish onion, diced
2 bags of spinach (about 400g)

3 tablespoons double cream
salt and freshly ground black pepper

METHOD

1. Heat the olive oil and fry the onion until it is soft and golden brown. Place the contents of the pan in a food-processor and process until smooth. Set aside.
2. Wash the spinach and cook very briefly in a dry pan with a lid – the residual water from the washing should be enough. Strain through a sieve, pressing out the juice, then place on a board and chop as finely as possible.
3. Put the spinach and the fried onion purée into a bowl, season, mix thoroughly and use the cream to bind the mixture together. Just before serving, heat the mixture in a pan to allow the flavours to blend.

PURPLE SPROUTING BROCCOLI WITH PINE NUTS AND RAISINS

Serves 4

2 bunches of purple sprouting broccoli
50ml olive oil
50g pine nuts, toasted in a dry pan

25g raisins, soaked for over 30 minutes in warm water

METHOD

1. Break the purple sprouting broccoli into individual stems and blanch briefly in salted boiling water. Drain carefully.
2. Heat the oil in a wok, add the sprouting (beware of spluttering!), pine nuts and soaked raisins and toss well together. Serve.

POLLO AL AJILLO WITH WHITE BEANS

Like so many recipes, this dish of Clare's draws from more than one source – one of which is the excellent recipe for pollo al ajillo that is to be found in Sam and Sam Clark's *Moro the Cookbook*, published by Ebury Press. But while holidaying in the village of Albuñuelas to the south of Granada, Clare fell in love with a similar garlic-laden dish that was made with rabbit and white beans. Out with the rabbit, in with the chicken and 'pollo al ajillo with white beans' is the happy result.

Serves 4

2 heads garlic	200ml white wine
50ml olive oil	100ml water
1 free range chicken, jointed	200g cooked cannellini beans (if using tinned
salt and freshly ground black pepper	beans rinse well)
6 bay leaves	

METHOD

1. Split the garlic heads into cloves without peeling them. Heat the oil in a deep pan and fry the garlic cloves gently until they are soft. Remove with a straining spoon and set aside.

2. Season the chicken pieces with salt and pepper and then fry in the garlic-flavoured oil for 10–15 minutes until they are golden and crisp. Shake the pan to stop them sticking and turn as necessary. Add the bay leaves and the garlic, plus the wine and water.

3. Cook gently for 15–25 minutes until the chicken is cooked through, then add the cannellini beans and cook for a further 5–10 minutes (you need the beans to warm through but hold their shape). If you want you can strain the sauce into a second pan to thicken it before turning in to a serving dish. Clare served this dish with roast carrots and a delicious purple sprouting broccoli dish.

LEMON CREAMS WITH AMARETTO MACAROONS

A good, rich and invigorating pudding, Clare credits Mary Berry's *Ultimate Cake Book* as the starting point for her macaroon recipe, while the addition of Amaretto liqueur makes them even more gooey in the middle.

Serves 4

For the lemon cream	For the macaroons
80g caster sugar	2 egg whites
227g double cream	100g ground almonds
juice and zest of 2 lemons	175g caster sugar
	25g plain flour
	splash of Amaretto liqueur

METHOD

1. First make the lemon creams. Put the sugar and cream into a saucepan and bring to the boil, then turn the heat down and cook gently for 3 minutes. Add as much lemon juice and zest as you like – using both the lemons will give a pleasantly tart cream that is a good contrast to the macaroons. Transfer to individual dishes and put in the refrigerator to firm up a little.

2. While the lemon creams are chilling, make the macaroons. Preheat the oven to 150°C/300°F/gas mark 2 and line a large baking tray with silicone paper. Whisk the egg whites to soft peaks, then fold in the almonds, sugar, flour and Amaretto. Mix well while trying to preserve the fluffiness of the beaten egg whites.

3. Drop teaspoonfuls of the mixture onto the paper (there should be enough mix for 16 macaroons). Space them out well as they will spread. Bake for 20–25 minutes, until golden brown. Cool on the tray for 5 minutes, then transfer the macaroons to cooling racks. Use the macaroons as spoons to scoop up the lemon cream.

LUNCH WITH

MICHAEL RODHAM

OTLEY, WEST YORKSHIRE

THE ROW OF SMALL TERRACED HOUSES is on a gentle hill that leads up to the Chevin – the ridge of high ground that looms over Otley. These houses were probably built towards the end of the 19th century, long before every household had a car and wanted to park outside the front door, so now the street has become a parking nightmare. This is a place from which the residents would have walked to work and the long terrace has several ginnels (the local term for an alley) so it's easy to cut through from street to street.

Michael Rodham lives mid-terrace and his house hides a secret. From the outside his home is much the same as all the others, a narrow cottage with a room to the front and one to the rear divided by the staircase – this really is 'two-up, two-down'. Michael opens the front door and you step straight off the street into an immaculately tidy front room, through to the back of the house and there's a small kitchen, but still no clues as to what is hidden in the cellar.

Michael is a remarkable fellow and manages to combine equal parts of passion and stubbornness. He has dug out the cellar and built himself a brewery. While most folk would be happy dabbling with a gallon or two of home brew, Michael has a set-up that is capable of making 2^1/2 barrels every two or three weeks (for metric folk unused to the vagaries of barrels, kilderkins, firkins and pins, that represents ten nine-gallon 'firkins' or 720 pints). He never set out to be a brewer; his first career was in credit control but he didn't like the people he was dealing with and sensibly enough that put him off the job.

Currently he works three or four days a week for Leeds Council. Temple Newsam may be unique in that it is an elegant council-owned stately home, complete with grand house, gardens, woods and a farm specialising in rare breeds. Michael works there helping teams of volunteers with the conservation tree planting programme – which means that his other job of brewing, cleaning, filling and labelling bottles and delivering barrels must be crammed into evenings, weekends and days off.

Like most people I find myself asking whether Otley Council was aware of his cottage industry – surely setting up an enterprise on this scale in your cellar must fall foul of some bureaucratic imperatives. Apparently not. Michael wrote a formal letter to the council and cited a precedent – a few years previously another Otley resident had marketed his home brew in local pubs and they had allowed him to continue brewing. The council had little option but grant permission, subject only to the strict condition that the brewery was in no way visible to the front or rear of the house. Council photographers have been round to snap pictures but the brewery is perfectly camouflaged. An unexpected by-product of the form filling is that the council health inspectors have been round and inspected the operation as if it were a restaurant: Michael was pleased to be awarded four stars out five for food hygiene even though he sells no food.

The regulations imposed by Her Majesty's Customs and Excise are equally complex. Michael has had a visit from the Duty men who were very picky; there's a lot of paperwork goes into calculating the duty payable on a humble pint and one key factor is ullage. This is the name for the amount of beer left sloshing around in the bottom of the barrel when you have drawn off all the delicious drinkable stuff. You have to pay duty on what is consumed but the ullage gets poured down the drain. Michael made a guess and claimed 500ml of ullage per barrel. The duty men first made him pay back all the duty claimed on the basis that the figure had not been approved. Then they calculated precisely what he was entitled to claim and came up with the figure of 900ml per barrel. So they rapped his knuckles and then awarded him an allowance nearly twice as large as the one he had claimed.

A brewing business, particularly a one-man brewing business, means plenty of hard work. Rodham's Brewery fills two rooms in the cellar: in one four-metre square room there's an array of stainless steel vats, a single water tap and a barrel washing area in the old coal hole. The other room is man made. It took Michael weeks to dig out the cellar that extends under the pavement and right up to his neighbour's party wall. As he excavated each bucket of earth it had to be winched up the cellar steps for dispersal in the back garden – the tunnellers involved in the 'Great Escape' may have had it easier. This is where barrels of beer mature, and houses the bottling machine (it fills three at a time). It's his pride and joy, but it still has such a low ceiling that he feels happier wearing a hard hat to soften the inevitable collisions with the rafters supporting the floor above.

When I asked him how he got the finished beer out of this tiny, cramped windowless cellar he replied that he walked the firkins up the stairs. That means putting your feet either side of the barrel and lifting it up a step, then moving your feet up and repeating the manoeuvre until you get to the cellar head. A full nine-gallon firkin of beer weighs 112lb (that's 51kg), so lifting it up twenty steps calls for serious stamina. 'When you're halfway up you wonder what you're doing it for, but when you get to the top it's all worthwhile,' he says. I make a comment that it still sounds like hard work, and in all seriousness Michael replies that it's not so bad as he can only get six barrels into his people carrier for delivery and thus only has to hump the barrels upstairs in batches of six. He thinks that bottling is a worse job – in an evening's bottling and labelling session – fill and cap each bottle then stick on a front and back label – he will do twenty dozen bottles.

Michael makes several different styles of beer but they all have one thing in common: they use the very best ingredients available – Maris Otter malt and First Gold hops. Rodham's India Pale Ale is a wacking 6.2 per cent alcohol on draught and 5.7 per cent when bottle conditioned – it's a magnificent beer, crisp and with a refreshing bitterness. Michael also makes a beguiling, clear, wheat beer; a rare, very dark beer called Old Albion, which beer purists would classify as a black lager; and two other brews called Rubicon and Royale, which are only available on draft. They are all well made and very drinkable indeed.

You only have to look around the tiny but tidy brewery operation to know what kind of a cook Michael Rodham will be – he is a meticulous man and before starting any dish he would certainly have everything worked out. We have lunch in the kitchen and start with an impromptu tasting of all his bottled beers (consuming enough rather good beer to add a rosy glow to the proceedings). He serves a simple venison casserole that he made the day before so that the flavours could develop overnight. It contains a bottle of his hoppy IPA and is very good. After lunch I leave and he waves goodbye from the doorway of his little terraced house, which looks very like every other house in the street. Perhaps there are hundreds of hidden breweries all over Britain? That's a pleasant thought.

VENISON CASSEROLED IN IPA

Michael Rodham devotes most of his time to recipes for making the beer itself rather than dreaming up cunning ways to use his beer in the kitchen, but this simple casserole really hits the spot. The India Pale Ale is a strong, well-hopped beer and the contrast between the sweetness of the fried onions and the bitterness of the beer is the making of the dish.

Serves 4

2 rashers smoked streaky bacon
500g pie venison
plain flour
knob of butter
150g onions, finely sliced
150g button mushrooms, halved

150g red peppers, deseeded and chopped
1 teaspoon dried thyme leaves
350ml India Pale Ale
350ml vegetable stock
salt and freshly ground black pepper

METHOD

1. Preheat the oven to 180°C/350°F/gas mark 4. Cut the bacon into lardons and fry until they release some fat. Roll the venison pieces in seasoned flour (cutting any that look larger than bite-size into two) then add to the pan and fry until browned. Remove the bacon and venison from the pan and pop it into a casserole dish.
2. Add the butter to the pan and fry the onions, mushrooms and peppers until they are softened and beginning to colour. Sprinkle with the dried thyme and add them to the casserole.
3. Rinse the frying pan with the beer to free up any crispy bits and add the liquid to the casserole. Add the vegetable stock (by all means make it with a stock cube but use only two thirds of the water suggested on the packet). Season with salt and freshly ground black pepper, then cook in the oven for about 90 minutes. Remove from the oven and leave to cool. Refrigerate overnight if possible, as this allows the flavours to mingle.
4. To serve, heat the casserole to boiling point and thicken the gravy with some cornflour if you think it necessary. Taste, and then adjust the seasoning. Serve with buttery mashed potato.

A MACROBIOTIC DINNER WITH

ALBERT MOSS
AND FRIENDS

BURNOPFIELD, COUNTY DURHAM

ALBERT MOSS has lived a busy and eventful life. He worked his way from an apprenticeship as a sheet metal worker in Byker, Newcastle Upon Tyne, to owning his own thriving engineering business. Albert freely admits that he has had his share of lucky breaks, but you cannot help noticing that his lucky breaks seem inextricably linked to hard work.

When you next walk up those endless airport corridors between the check-in and the departure gates keep your eyes open and you might spot the foundation of Albert's fortune. The 120-odd people who worked in Albert's factory spent a large proportion of their time making the red painted steel cabinets that house fire hoses and extinguishers. Eventually Albert tired of the business life and sold his company, at which point he bought a smallholding and went self-sufficient.

As is typical of someone so fiercely driven, this was not a hobbyist 'Good Life' experiment but an uncompromising venture – the farm produced goat's milk, hen's eggs, lamb, rabbits, vegetables, fruit, the works. What's more, Albert will tell you proudly that he never used chemicals on his land and has always stuck rigidly to biodynamic principles.

The farm is scaled back now, although the neat rows of immaculate vegetables still march across a large and flourishing vegetable patch as Albert sets about his latest challenge. In 2008 Albert Moss was diagnosed as having prostate cancer. What's more, the initial treatment was not successful and the cancer spread through his body. It was a turning point for Albert and he decided to fight. 'I was determined to take the matter into my own hands. I read extensively about self-healing through food, and set about curing myself.' When you look across the kitchen at Albert as he cooks dinner you cannot fail to notice how neat, precise and determined a cook he is – measurements are exact and if his notes say that he should be cutting the beetroot into 1cm squares, you can bet that's the exact size they end up.

Albert Moss has gone macrobiotic. Once a week his macrobiotic counsellor Paul Lambeth stops by to help answer any queries and to give Albert a shiatsu massage session. It is hard to summarise the principles of an entire philosophy and way of life, but for the layman it seems that the key features of the macrobiotic diet are avoiding all kinds of animal protein – meat, butter, cheese; also plants from the nightshade (solanaceae) family – tomatoes, potatoes, peppers, aubergines; also spinach and avocados. This leaves a shopping list of wholegrain cereals, fresh vegetables (best used as soon after picking as possible), seaweed, fermented soy products like tofu, fish in moderation, buckwheat, beans and pulses. It's all very well but how do you go about turning out a macrobiotic dinner party?

Albert's menu was long and complicated and it's worth mentioning at the outset that the meal was a great success. Varied tastes, varied textures and a surprising degree of sophistication. Before dinner the canapés were made from little discs of polenta soda bread topped with a green pea and walnut pâté. The bread was very light and open-textured and the pâté had a pleasant nutty crunch. The first course was a light miso soup with ginger, toasted sesame oil and spring onions. This was a rich-tasting bowlful that made an excellent job of kicking the taste buds into life. Then Albert served a green salad, with roasted beetroot, cubes of smoked tofu and an orange dressing – this was a great success, a grand balance of textures set off by the sweet-sharp orange dressing. The 'first' main course was a seitan cutlet and although I am instinctively distrustful of the merits of vegetables prodded and poked into faux meat, I must admit the strange, chewy but firm texture of the seitan worked well with the crispy coating. The other substantial dish was a bowl of brown rice enlivened by shiitake mushrooms, onions, garlic and shoyu soy.

You could tell that the other guests at the dinner table were not familiar with macrobiotic food, if only by their surprised expression as each dish came to table. The collective verdict was, 'I wasn't expecting food this good.' It was a salutary exercise in the way that good cooking can make the most of what at first seems like an unpromising selection of ingredients.

Is it possible that a macrobiotic diet can indeed combat cancer? When you meet Albert Moss you cannot fail to notice that he has an iron will, the kind of inner strength that can achieve a great deal. When he started his macrobiotic diet Albert had a PSA of 36 (this is a measure that quantifies prostate cancer), after six months of staying away from conventional medicine and whole-hearted macrobiotic living that figure was reduced to 0.8.

One of Albert's favourite quotes is a one liner from Hippocrates (the father of modern medicine, born in 460BC on the Greek island of Cos): 'Let food be thy medicine and medicine be thy food.' Albert believes this passionately and he is putting it into practice.

POLENTA SODA BREAD

This bread has a remarkably open and cake-like texture that belies its savoury taste. Cut discs from thin slices and use them as canapé bases.

Makes 1 medium loaf

300g fine polenta	2 teaspoons sea salt
200g spelt flour	100ml corn oil
3 teaspoons baking powder	150ml soya cream
1 teaspoon bicarbonate of soda	250ml soya milk

METHOD

1. Preheat the oven to 160°C/325°F/gas mark 3. Oil a rectangular loaf tin, about 23x13x7cm – the mixture will not fill this size of tin but it will leave room for the bread to rise.
2. Mix the polenta, spelt, baking powder, bicarbonate of soda and salt together in a large mixing bowl. Mix the corn oil, soya cream and soya milk in a jug, then add to the dry ingredients, stirring everything together until you have a sloppy batter; if it looks too thick, add a little water until you have a very soft consistency.
3. Pour into the prepared tin and bake in the centre of the oven for an hour – the bread is done when a skewer plunged into the centre comes out clean.

GREEN PEA AND WALNUT PÂTÉ

This is a very light and fresh pâté that is like a superior houmous.

Serves 4 as a starter

75g walnut kernels	1 teaspoon miso
125g fresh peas (or frozen peas)	freshly ground black pepper and
1 tablespoon olive oil	sea salt
1 large onion, finely chopped	juice of 1 lemon

METHOD

1. Dry roast the walnuts in a frying pan. If you are using fresh peas, blanch them in boiling water for 3 minutes and pop them into a bowl of cold water to fix the green colour. If you are using frozen peas this stage has been taken care of.
2. Heat the olive oil and cook the onion until soft but not coloured.
3. Put the toasted walnuts, peas, onions and miso into a blender or food-processor and whizz until you have a pâté but be careful not to overdo it. Season to taste with pepper, sea salt and a squeeze of lemon, then whizz some more until mixed.

GREEN SALAD WITH ROASTED BEETROOT, SMOKED TOFU AND ORANGE DRESSING

A simple green salad kicked into life by the addition of roasted beetroot, chunks of savoury tasting smoked tofu and a perky orange dressing.

Serves 4

200g smoked tofu
6 small beetroot
150ml shoyu soy sauce
50ml olive oil
lots of green leaves, e.g. lettuce, mesclun or whatever takes your fancy

For the dressing

18 oranges or 2 tablespoons concentrated orange juice
2 tablespoons agave syrup
3 tablespoons rice vinegar
2 tablespoons shoyu soy sauce

METHOD

1. First make the dressing. Juice the oranges and heat in a pan until reduced to 3–4 tablespoons of concentrated orange juice. Combine with the other ingredients in a jar with a tightly fitting lid (so that you can shake it to mix). Adjust the seasoning with shoyu soy and Agave syrup to taste.
2. Cut the smoked tofu into 1cm cubes and mix gently with the shoyu. Leave to marinate for at least 1 hour.
3. Preheat the oven to 180°C/350°F/gas mark 4. Roast the beetroot on a tray for about 30 minutes until cooked. Set aside to cool.
4. Heat the olive oil in a frying pan and cook the tofu until a pleasing crust forms on each side.
5. Slip the skins from the beetroot and chop into 1cm dice. In a large bowl toss the leaves, tofu and beetroot in the orange dressing, then serve immediately.

LIGHT MISO SOUP WITH GINGER, TOASTED SESAME OIL AND SPRING ONIONS

Miso soup is a wonderfully versatile dish and one that features strongly in Albert's regime – he often has it for breakfast and claims that it has awesome powers of invigoration! You can tailor it to suit the occasion at which it is served – this recipe is for a strongly flavoured elegant soup but should a winter's day demand a heartier, more substantial soup simply treble the amount of vegetables added.

Serves 4

For the stock	*For the soup*
2 large carrots	300g jar of barley miso (Clearspring Onozake
2 sticks celery	Organic Barley Miso is a name worth noting)
2 large onions	1 carrot, cut into matchstick batons
75g root ginger, peeled and cut into chunks	1 turnip, cut into matchstick batons
1 litre water	75g French beans, cut into 2cm lengths
	1 tablespoon toasted sesame oil
	6 spring onions, finely chopped (use both
	the white and green parts)

METHOD

1. Start by making the vegetable stock. Chop the carrots, celery and onions into fine dice, put them in a large pot, add the ginger, bring to the boil and then simmer for 30 minutes. Feel free to add other fresh vegetables. Strain off the vegetables and work on the soup.
2. Put 250ml of the stock into a bowl, dissolve the miso into it, then return to the main pan. From this point the stock should never boil. Add the matchstick vegetables and simmer very gently until they are hot through and starting to cook but are still crunchy. Stir in the sesame oil. Add the spring onions and serve.

SEITAN CUTLETS PAN-FRIED WITH A HERB AND BREADCRUMB CRUST

Seitan is strange stuff. It is sometimes known as 'wheat meat' and is a popular weapon in the vegetarian chef's armoury. It is made from flour (somewhat laboriously) and derives its texture and character from the gluten found in wheat flour. Seitan is becoming more popular and you can often find it ready made next to the tofu in your local health food shop.

Makes about 1kg of seitan

2kg strong white bread flour
water (blood temperature)
100g root ginger, peeled and sliced
200ml shoyu soy sauce

For the herb and breadcrumb crust
100g plain white flour
200ml water
fresh rosemary, thyme and sage,
finely chopped
white breadcrumbs
sesame oil, for frying

METHOD

1. Put the flour into a large bowl. Using a jug, gradually add the water as you work the flour into a dough. Knead for at least 10 minutes (the dough is ready when you push a finger into it and the indentation remains and doesn't pop out). Put the ball of dough into a clean bowl and cover it with warm water. Set aside for at least an hour to prove.

2. Cut chunks the size of a cricket ball from the dough. Work each one with your hands (breaking it and re-forming it) under a running tap. At the beginning of this process the water will run cloudy with starch; as you proceed the water will run clear – a sign that the starch has gone and the gluten remains. Re-form all the balls into 1 big lump.

3. Put the lump of seitan into a pressure cooker with the ginger, top up with the shoyu and barely cover with water. Cook under full pressure for 30 minutes – the dough will swell up. Allow to cool, then cut the seitan into 'cutlets' about 2cm thick.

4. To make the crust, first mix the flour and the 200ml of water to make a light batter. Mix together the chopped herbs and breadcrumbs.
5. Coat the seitan slices in the batter, and then in the breadcrumb mix. Fry in sesame oil until nicely brown.

BROWN RICE WITH FRESH SHIITAKE MUSHROOMS, ONIONS, PEAS AND FRESH PARSLEY

Nutty and satisfying, this dish works well because of the contrasting textures of the rice and peas and the balance between the savoury shoyu soy and the shiitake mushrooms.

Serves 4

3 tablespoons sesame oil
1 onion, finely diced
200g fresh shiitake mushrooms, sliced
1 large garlic clove, finely chopped
200g fresh peas, podded
1 teaspoon sea salt

shoyu soy sauce
mirin
350g brown rice (cooked with 1 teaspoon sea salt)
shiitake seasoning (available from health food shops)
finely chopped fresh parsley, to garnish

METHOD

1. Heat the oil in a frying pan and cook the onion and mushrooms together until the onions turn translucent and the mushrooms give up their water. Add the garlic and cook a little further. Add the peas and the salt. When you are sure that you have cooked out as much water as possible, add the shoyu and mirin until you have a strongly flavoured mix.
2. Fold the shiitake mixture into the rice until all is amalgamated – be careful to do this gently and thus avoid mashing the rice grains. Add a little more sesame oil if necessary. Dress the rice with shiitake seasoning and the chopped parsley.

THE NOSE

Edinburgh

IF YOU KNOCKED ON THE DOOR OF CENTRAL CASTING and asked if they could recommend the archetypal Scotsman – bristling moustache, aquiline profile, gimlet-eyed, ruddy complexion, the kind of legs that look good in a kilt – they would get straight on the phone to Charlie MacLean. As a bonus Charlie is one of those gently spoken cerebral Scots; he may be full of passion but it is underpinned by intellect. Whisky is his life's passion and his enthusiasm alone is enough to convert fervent whisky haters into whisky lovers.

Charles MacLean came to whisky by a roundabout route. He started by chalking up a degree in divinity and art history at the University of St Andrew's, followed by a law degree from Dundee, which flowered into a brief stint working as a solicitor in Edinburgh – he holds the rather obscure office of 'Writer to the Queen's Signet', a 16th-century title that lingers on in Scottish jurisprudence. A chance encounter with Alexander McCall Smith in the 1970s, at an Edinburgh debating club called the Speculative Society, led to his abandoning the law and setting up a literary agency called MacLean Dubois. MacLean is a very real character but Dubois is a fiction, the second name being added to the masthead in order to add substance. The mission statement of the agency was to find all the brilliant writers scattered across the remoter parts of Scotland and get them the recognition they deserved. In practice MacLean Dubois took but a single step into the big time, a book about the Yorkshire Ripper written by Roger Cross. During the 1980s Charlie turned his hand to writing and had various books published ranging from *The Clans of Scotland* to *Get to Know the Forests of Northern England*. Then he was asked to write the centenary brochure for the Highland Distilleries and, fascinated by the historical research involved and with a growing appreciation of the subtleties of whisky, he changed tack and started to specialise. In 1993 he wrote the Mitchell Beazley *Pocket Whisky Book*, which is still recognised as a classic.

This love affair with whisky might only have been a one-night stand were it not for a classic 'lucky break'. Charlie MacLean secured a place on an ultra-specialist short course at Heriot-Watt University, this was set up by Pentlands Scotch Whisky Research (which organisation went on to become the Scotch Whisky Research Institute), and was aimed at the production managers of whisky companies. This unlikely sounding Road to Damascus was entitled 'the sensory evaluation of potable spirits'.

Charlie MacLean acknowledges that it was a genuinely life-changing experience. 'It was astonishing, rather like growing an extra limb. Learning to distinguish and analyse aromas opened an entire new world. I would come back from the course and go into the kitchen, I couldn't resist smelling the waste bin – before it was just rubbish, but now I could pick out the aroma of the banana skins and that empty baked bean tin.'

Evaluating whisky is a complex and challenging business and it is one where the sense of smell plays the crucial part. We are all exposed to a barrage of different smells every minute of the day, but our sense of smell is at once the least understood and most powerful of our senses. The olfactory nerve communicates directly with the limbic system, which is a primitive part of the brain and is also the seat of emotion and memory. Thus information about each and every smell has a direct route to our inner being and arrives there unmediated. Perhaps that is why encountering any scent from our childhood – newly mown grass or freshly baked biscuits – provokes such a surge of memories? Charlie is fond of quoting Diane Ackerman's book *A Natural History of the Senses*, 'Nothing is more memorable than the smell. Smells detonate in our memory like poignant landmines.' When it comes to trying different whiskies aroma is more important than taste, and the professional blenders rarely put the whisky in their mouths – no wonder they are called 'noses'.

Charlie MacLean makes a key distinction between enjoying whisky and appreciating it. 'If you enjoy drinking whisky with coke and ice, so be it. But if you are keen to appreciate whisky and get more out of it, there are simple guidelines that will enhance the experience.' It's simple really, everything that works with aroma is good while everything that reduces the impact of the aroma is bad. So, choose a glass that has an appropriate deep bowl for swirling the whisky around to release the aroma, but the glass should also taper to a narrow top to funnel the aromas to your nose. No ice. It reduces the aroma – room temperature is fine. Then, when you have swirled and sniffed to your heart's content, add water. All those macho heroes who proclaim that 'the only way to drink whisky is neat' have got it wrong. Diluting whisky with water will not only release the flavours and aromas, but also reduce 'nose prickle', that eye-watering, aroma-hampering kick you get from neat spirits. As a duffer's guide, whisky with a strength of 40 per cent needs 'up to the same amount of water again'. Always remember to swirl your water in a jug and 'nose' it before adding it to the whisky – if your tap water smells of chlorine, or any other chemical taint, you're best off adding bottled water to your precious single malt.

For over a decade Charlie MacLean has chaired the tasting panel for the Scotch Malt Whisky Society. This is the committee that decides which casks the Society should buy, and he trains future panel members in the arcane skill of sensory evaluation. He is firmly of the opinion that everyone can learn to taste, as we are all similarly equipped at a physiological level, but he concedes that women are often slightly better tasters than men. This is something that he puts down to the greater exposure they get to aromas in their day-to-day lives. From an aromatic perspective, malt whisky is the most complex spirit of all, and it could be argued that the 'nose' plays an even greater part than it does when tasting fine wines. With blended whiskies the aim is to combine a variety of characteristics so that the whole is greater than the sum of its parts and that means fewer intense aromas and more emphasis on flavour. (Aroma is olfactory, while flavour is more taste-driven).

'Whisky is hugely complex and rewards attention, making every nuance worthy of consideration,' but when talking whisky Charlie shows that he is completely entranced by the romance of the stuff and its interesting and long history. As he says, 'It appeals to a Scot,' and is still a very natural product with a very short list of ingredients – malted barley, water and yeast. In that respect it is very similar to bread-making; you start with a few staples and you end up with something that is both simple and delicious. The joy of this endeavour is that whether you are talking malt whiskies or hand-baked loaves there can be an unlimited range of different outcomes even when you start with identical ingredients. It is important that we value these craft-made products and ancient processes.

One of the great joys of whisky is that no-one knows exactly how great whisky is made. The scientist may have gained many more insights during the last decade or so, but they still cannot explain why you can set up a brand new plant alongside an existing old-established distillery, and the spirit from each will be different. So it would seem that the French wine makers' concept of 'terroir' doesn't have as much impact for the whisky makers. Although the influence of tradition (i.e. 'We've always done it this way in this glen!') does make a difference. This inability to find the foolproof scientific explanation as to why the whisky produced at different distilleries varies so much is something that irritates the businessmen in charge of the whisky industry. What they long for is consistency: they would like every batch of white spirit produced by a particular distillery to be much the same. But the baleful influence of accountants – they were particularly influential during the 1970s and 1980s – has left an industry that is misguidedly striving to be more industrial and less romantic. It is also interesting to note that 90 per cent of the whisky produced in Scotland ends up being drunk abroad – this is primarily an export business.

If you ask Charlie MacLean about pairing food and whisky he takes the view that this makes a good way to introduce more people to whisky and make them more aware of the variety that is on offer. It also has the benefit of making people taste things carefully. Foodies know that trying wine with different foods 'alters' the taste of the wine and the same is true of whisky. This is something you can prove for yourself by taking the 'Tequila test' – line up three wines, a white, a rosé and a red. Try them all. Then taste a pinch of salt before trying them again. Finally, suck the lime and then try the wines. You will find that the perceived character of the wines changes depending on the flavours with which you accompany them. In similar fashion, by trying malts with foods that have different characteristics you can showcase flavours in the whiskies that were not previously apparent. As an illustration Charlie nominates the unlikely sounding marriage of Lagavulin (an oily, smoky, fruity, island whisky) and Roquefort (a strident, blue, salty and intensely flavoured ewe's milk cheese). Here two magnificent heavyweight flavours clash and bring out the best in each other. Perhaps we'll soon see the whisky decanter passed around with the cheese board?

It is interesting to speculate whether whisky tasting is closer to wine tasting or beer tasting. What is certain is that the whisky lovers tend to be drawn from all strata of society whereas the attendees at a wine tasting tend to be slightly more upmarket and those attending beer festivals tend to be single-minded. Charlie has a great respect for the knowledgeable whisky fans, particularly those on the Continent where he describes the audiences at his whisky tastings as 'everyone from bankers to bikers, but all remarkably well informed'.

I never liked whisky until Charlie MacLean sat me down and made me pay attention. I followed his directives about using the right glass, swirling and sniffing; adding the right amount of water and so avoiding the dread 'nose prickle' and in a trice everything changed. The range of different aromas and flavours is truly eye-opening and it is delightful to find that there might be a 'morning whisky', an 'afternoon whisky' and a 'late night whisky'. I like the arcane and flowery language – now that I can detect the aromas they describe. At a stroke I had moved from being a drinker to an appreciator and could even consider a phrase like 'sensory evaluation of potable spirits' without glassing over.

Malt whisky has no better ambassador than Charlie MacLean. He is knowledgeable, passionate, resolutely Scottish, and into the bargain he has an incredibly highly tuned nose.

LUNCH WITH
MERLYN RIGGS
INVERURIE, ABERDEENSHIRE

BY ANY MEASURE, Merlyn Riggs is pretty fierce. The jolly tones, the scarlet
and ginger hair and the ebullient personality cannot disguise the glint in her eye
and a passion·for righting society's wrongs. When asked about her unusual name
she laughs and mentions that her father had a penchant for the quirky. Family
lore has it that she had been within a hair's breadth of having the middle name of
Arthur in honour of her grandfather. To a girl who could have been named Arthur,
Merlyn must seem a pretty ordinary sort of name. After snagging an honours
degree in sculpture at Aberdeen University Merlyn became fascinated by 'social
sculpture', a discipline refined by an influential German artist called Joseph Beuys
in the post-war years. To the layman, social sculpture seems to lie somewhere
between performance art and avant garde installations. Merlyn describes it as
'making an ephemeral sculpture, but instead of working with hard materials I use
people.' She also proudly admits that she is 'an activist on women's issues' and
hopes all her projects make a contribution to the greater cause.

Many of the projects rely on her cooking skills and she certainly made her present
felt with one such event set up to highlight the imbalance that still exists between

the sexes. Merlyn invited a group of twenty members of the university staff (ten women and ten men) to come for 'coffee and cakes' one afternoon. They arrived on cue and settled down to enjoy their coffee while Merlyn made a speech about the cakes, saying how wonderful they were and describing how glorious and delicious they would taste – she describes this as 'giving them the full Nigella'. When the audience was dribbling in anticipation she announced that the cake was only for the women. This neat reversal of the tradition whereby the male head of the household is always deferred to at the dinner table caused uproar. Two gentlemen stormed out. One lady offered to smuggle a slice of cake over to another gentleman. To underline the point a vote was taken among the women and it was made official, no cake for the men.

Merlyn lives with her husband Rabb in a pretty cottage tucked away off the road among some trees. There's a higgledy-piggledy jumble of herbs and growbags outside and a vast kitchen sprawling through the middle of the house. To one end of the room are the cages of two African Grey parrots – and yes, they do have a repertoire of unsuitable words plus the uncanny knack of screaming them at the most inappropriate moment. The household is completed by a platoon of seven cats; their mission is to try and catch the parrots when they are allowed out of their cages for exercise – to date they have not succeeded.

Merlyn is a good cook and makes great use of local ingredients. We started with one of the great iconic Scottish dishes, Cullen Skink and it was suitably thick and satisfying – it's amazing how a simple flavour like smoked haddock can be used to gently infuse a whole bowl of soup, but this is a subtle matter that demands expertise from the cook as too much of that flavour is as much a problem as too little. The main course was venison in a pastry parcel, again local, and teamed with black pudding and brambles scrumped from local woods. With it came a dish of skirlie (partly because I had expressed curiosity about this Scottish classic). While you can eat it on its own, I have included Merlyn's recipe for butternut squash stuffed with skirlie, which is a real winner. By way of side dishes Merlyn cooked some tomatoes down to a rich and chunky salsa and also prepared some Savoy cabbage – shredded and stir-fried with tiny wedges of lemon – very good indeed. For pudding there was a glorious fluffy, creamy concoction on a cheesecake-style base and topped with raspberries that had been marinated in a little whisky.

Giving the lie to anyone brought up to think of Scottish gastronomy as stumbling from porridge to haggis and back again, this meal delivered distinct flavours and well balanced textures. Honest food but with some sophisticated touches and with an admirable sense of place. But when you're aware of Merlyn's penchant for social sculpture you do look at every course wondering if there is some hidden agenda that is going to leap out and bite you. Then again, approaching a meal with a little more respect may be no bad thing!

CULLEN SKINK

Sometimes dishes are so iconic and famous that everyone has an opinion about how they should be made. Cullen Skink is just such a dish and you may find it re-branded on chic menus as 'haddock chowder'. Skink originated in the fishing village of Cullen, a little way to the north of Aberdeen, and has an admirably short ingredient list. Merlyn's version is a soup that thinks it's a stew or perhaps the other way around. The 'Finnan Haddie' should be undyed and for the perfect texture the potatoes should be waxy rather than floury.

Serves 4

450g smoked haddock	25g unsalted butter (plus some for the dish)
300ml whole milk	25g plain flour
2 large onions, finely chopped	400ml fish stock (or chicken stock at a pinch –
2 large waxy potatoes, sliced very thinly	supermarket stock will do fine)
freshly ground black pepper	snipped chives, for garnish (optional)

METHOD

1. Preheat the oven to 180°C/350°F/gas mark 4. Butter a flat pie dish. If the smoked haddock is a very thick fillet, poach it in the milk for 3 minutes. Strain, reserving the milk, and set aside. Skin the fish and flake it. If the haddock fillet is thinner omit the poaching stage and just skin and flake the fish.
2. Layer the onions, potatoes and fish in the dish and add the milk. Season with black pepper (the haddock should provide enough salt). Bake for 40 minutes or until the potato is soft.
3. Towards the end of this time, melt the butter in a pan, stir in the flour and cook gently for 1–2 minutes. Add the fish stock, gradually working it in as you go. You should end up with a runny sauce. Season to taste and keep piping hot.
4. To serve, put a dollop of the fish, onion and potato mix into each bowl and add the sauce so that the fish becomes an 'island'. You can dress with a few snipped chives if you wish.

VENISON AND BRAMBLE 'GENERAL GORDON'

Were we south of the border this dish would certainly be called a venison Wellington, but it seems appropriate to credit a famous Scottish general. You can make this dish with venison fillet, but in the interests of expediency and economy venison steaks (do be sure that they are cut thickly) work pretty well. The brambles add a sweet tang and the mix lubricates the venison, which could otherwise end up a tad dry. Shop-bought all-butter shortcrust pastry is perfect for this job, but by way of a warning, Merlyn has tried, and failed, to replicate the dish with filo.

Serves 4

50g unsalted butter	salt and freshly ground black pepper
1 large red onion, very finely chopped	1 dram whisky
1 garlic clove, very finely chopped	4 thick pieces of venison fillet (about
1 tablespoon soft brown sugar	150g each)
a few sprigs of fresh thyme	500g all-butter shortcrust pastry
a few sprigs of fresh rosemary	1 egg, beaten
200g wild brambles	4 slices of black pudding, about 5mm thick

METHOD

1. Start by making the bramble and onion jam. Heat the butter in a pan, add the onion and the garlic and sweat for about 10 minutes. Add the sugar, herbs and brambles and cook slowly for 30–40 minutes until reduced to a jam. Season with salt and pepper and allow to cool. When cold stir in half the whisky.
2. Preheat the oven to 220°C/425°F/gas mark 7. Sear the venison in a very hot, dry pan. You need it to brown and for a crust to form; this should take less than a minute each side.
3. Roll out the pastry quite thinly and cut into four 15cm squares. Brush the edges with the beaten egg to help glue everything together. Spread a thick layer of bramble mixture in the centre, top with the venison, then a little more bramble and finally the black pudding. Bring the parcel together and seal carefully.
4. Brush the parcels with the egg and bake (timings are approximate depending on your oven) – 20 minutes should be rare, 26 minutes medium and 32 minutes well done. Check by cutting into the meat and having a peek. Rest for five minutes before serving.

SKIRLIE-STUFFED BUTTERNUT SQUASH

Think of skirlie as a sort of moody Scottish polenta! It's a staple grain (in this case oats) with added flavour due to some simple additions and a straightforward cooking method. Merlyn uses the pinhead 'Oatmeal of Alford' from the nearby Montgarrie Mill. The finished dish has a delightful crunchiness to it.

Serves 4

25g unsalted butter
25g dripping
1 large onion, finely chopped

150g pinhead oatmeal
salt and freshly ground pepper
4 small butternut squash

METHOD

1. Preheat the oven to 180°C/350°F/gas mark 4. Start by making the skirlie. Heat the butter and dripping in a pan and fry the onion gently until it is soft. Add the oatmeal and stir together, letting it soak up the juices. Season well.
2. Cut 'lids' off the squash and scoop out the seeds. Stuff with skirlie and put the lids back on, sealing everything up by wrapping tightly in foil. Bake until the squash is cooked (test with the point of a knife) – it should take about 35 minutes but you cannot overdo this dish.

CHEESELESS CRANACHAN 'CHEESECAKE'

Merlyn calls this dessert a cheesecake, but it is not baked and there is no sign of any cheese. And it's all the better for that, being a grand, light, almost fluffy sweet with a good contrast between the fruit, the crunchy base and the topping. The acidity of the lemon juice firms up the cream in much the same way as when preparing a posset. Make the cake in advance and then ladle on the raspberries as you serve. There have been rumours of people making this dessert with Hobnobs rather than digestives – it's unlikely to work as it probably ends up a tad too sweet.

Serves 4

400g fresh or frozen raspberries	100g unsalted butter, melted
2 drams of whisky	600ml double cream
25g icing sugar	juice of 2 lemons
50g large porridge oats	200g condensed milk
1 small packet digestive biscuits	2 tablespoons heather honey

METHOD

1. Start by marinating the raspberries (they will improve for anything up to 24 hours). Combine them with half the whisky and the icing sugar. Cover and refrigerate.
2. Toast the oatmeal: spread it out under the grill and watch it like a hawk, as it burns easily. The oatmeal is ready when crisp and nutty.
3. Crumble the biscuits and add the melted butter, working until it comes together. Pack the mixture into a 25cm flan tin to make a base.
4. Whip the cream until it starts to thicken but is not too firm, add the lemon juice, condensed milk, honey and remaining whisky, continuing to beat. Fold in the oats. Chill.
5. Spread the creamy mixture onto the base and chill once more. Cut each guest a slice and pour the raspberry mixture over the top.

DINNER WITH
SUZANNE, PAUL, TOD, MATT
AND THEO WASILOWSKI
WETHERAL, CUMBRIA

IN JUNE 2006 SUZANNE AND PAUL WASILOWSKI were both happy with their jobs in the motor trade, right up until the moment when they heard that the village post office in the picture postcard Cumbrian village of Wetheral was up for sale. Everything seemed to click into place: their next door neighbour knew the owner and in an indecently short time they had not only moved house but also changed careers. Wetheral is a plush little village just outside Carlisle and is home to a hotel, a pub and an old-established and well-regarded restaurant. When the Wasilowskis took over the village shop and post office it was the weak link in the chain and rather run down.

Fast forward to the present – after a great deal of hard work – and Suzanne describes it as somewhere that sells 'everything to everybody'. The small shop is crammed with food and drink; fresh bread comes from Bryson's of Keswick; there is a healthy emphasis on small regional suppliers; an expansive range of wines; and half the premises is let out to a local outdoor caterer who has set up a coffee lounge. The Wasilowskis have also taken on the mantle of newsagent, so the shop is open from 6.30am to 5.30pm for 363 days of the year (they close for Christmas Day and

New Year's Day). Suzanne has the imposing title of 'Postmistress' and this place is a perfect example of why we hope that the campaign to keep our rural post offices open succeeds.

Suzanne was brought up on a farm just north of the border between England and Scotland, her mother was a good cook and renowned for her fish pie. Fish pie was one of the first dishes Suzanne cooked for Paul, her then husband-to-be, and he confesses that some time later when he tried her mother's fish pie he shamelessly voted it 'better than Suzanne's', doing himself no harm in the son-in-law stakes. Farming is a hard way to make a living and involves an old-fashioned amount of physical work, which in turn leads to a need for large, regular meals and dishes that deliver plenty of energy. By the time she was ten Suzanne was making the supper for the family and was an accomplished baker.

You would have thought that such a valuable grounding would have made her somewhat dismissive of the current fixation with celebrity chefs but she readily confesses that the family were engrossed by Marco Pierre White's antics on Hell's Kitchen. Other favourites include James Martin, Rachel Allen and Jamie Oliver. Indeed, Paul admits that Jamie's Ministry of Food programmes prompted him to start doing some cooking himself. With three small boys to cater for – Tod, six, Matt, three, and Theo, bringing up the rear at eighteen months – and the demands of running the shop downstairs, Suzanne's style of cooking has evolved into a beguiling combination of very practical dishes that also deliver a good balance of flavours.

One of the pluses (and drawbacks) of being postmistress and living over the business is a tendency to treat the well-stocked shop downstairs as 'the biggest larder in the world' – it is very handy to pop down for a bottle of wine or some beers. The downside is that the whole family have discovered an appetite for sweets – everything from traditional boiled sweets to chocolate bars. Despite being a period piece, the television series Lark Rise to Candleford may have skewed our view of village postmistresses, but Suzanne is just as unruffled as her telly equivalent and radiates calm, while Wetheral Post Office has certainly become a hub of village life.

When we sit down to dinner with the two eldest boys the sensible nature of Suzanne's menu becomes apparent – the dish of mushrooms under a herb crust is not time sensitive, it is ready when we are; then the boys hit the fish pie with glee and by the time we get to dessert the local ice cream that is served with the raspberry and white chocolate sponge puddings delights them. It's not often you eat with such young children and get away with so little fussiness. Viewed from an adult perspective it's a delightful meal.

One of Suzanne's strengths is the way she takes one idea – while eating out in a restaurant she very much enjoyed a plate of mussels that had been cooked under a herb crust – and a few tweaks later she had developed the dish of creamy mushrooms under a similar herb and breadcrumb crust. It's a very good starter, rather like a 'mushroom crumble' if that doesn't sound too far fetched. The fish pie also delivers – rich and satisfying but with the fish cooked just about perfectly; in so many fish pies the fish has been cooked well past the point where it has any flavour or texture, but Suzanne's variation of the method resolves this problem. The pudding is also a considered dish: she has brought together fresh fruit and a traditional sponge pudding, but in such a way that it almost fringes on soufflé territory.

The final element of the meal doesn't really count as a recipe but does embody the spirit of the post office at Wetheral: a trio of local cheeses, served with rather delicious biscuits made by Carr's in Carlisle; a rich plum cake from Bryson's of Keswick and some home-made chutney. It may simply be raiding the larder downstairs, but it confirms a genuine attempt to stock some of the excellent products made locally, which is just what you would expect from a well-organised and talented cook like Suzanne Wasilowski.

MIXED MUSHROOMS UNDER A HERB CRUST

Suzanne has a soft spot for mushrooms and with a starting point of that old cliché 'garlic mushrooms' – a dish that has pride of place on a thousand pub menus – she has developed a more subtle and sophisticated recipe. This dish works well because it delivers two contrasting textures and the hint of garlic is tamed by fresh herbs. It is also an easy dish that can be prepared ahead of time and then re-heated and finished when needed.

Serves 4

50g unsalted butter
300g mixed mushrooms (e.g. flat field mushrooms, white button mushrooms, portobello or chestnut), cut into equal-sized pieces
1 garlic clove, peeled and crushed
large bunch fresh parsley, roughly chopped

$^1/_2$ glass white wine
3 tablespoons crème fraîche
salt and freshly ground black pepper
200g white bread (crusts removed)
50g Parmesan, grated
a few rocket leaves, to decorate

METHOD

1. Preheat the oven to 180°C/350°F/gas mark 4. Melt half the butter in a frying pan, add the mushrooms and garlic and cook until the mushrooms give up some of their water.
2. Add half the parsley to the pan with the wine and crème fraîche. Season with salt and pepper and set aside.
3. Place the white bread in a food processor and whizz, then add the Parmesan and the remaining butter and parsley. Whizz until it all comes together.
4. Divide the mushroom mixture between four shallow ovenproof dishes and top each with the breadcrumb mixture. Pat down and bake for 8–10 minutes until crispy and golden. Serve topped with a few rocket leaves by way of decoration and to add some colour.

FISH PIE

Ever since it gained welcome exposure on a succession of cookery programmes, fish pie has become an iconic dish. Suzanne's recipe is rather less fussy than most (when making my own my fish pie I usually start by poaching the fish in milk, lifting it out and then making the white sauce with the resulting fishy milk). But Suzanne starts by selecting fish that need less cooking (smoked cod, salmon fillet and cooked prawns), so she can put them into the pie uncooked. As a result she saves several stages. This makes for a very good fish pie – rich and comforting with the fish perfectly cooked. All it needs for accompaniment is a crisp green vegetable.

Serves 4

500g floury potatoes, peeled
generous knob of butter, plus extra for greasing
salt and freshly ground black pepper
180g skinless salmon fillet
180g skinless smoked cod fillet
80g cooked prawns

For the white sauce
400–500ml whole milk
70g butter
70g flour
1/2 glass white wine
150g cheddar cheese, grated
a little chopped fresh parsley

METHOD

1. Preheat the oven to 180°C/350°F/gas mark 4. Cook the potatoes in boiling water until soft, then mash with the butter (use as much as you like!) and season to taste.
2. Butter a large pie dish, add the fish cut into chunks and scatter prawns on top.
3. Make the white sauce. Heat the milk in a jug. Melt the butter in a pan, add the flour, stirring until you have a roux. Cook the mixture for a minute or so but do not allow it to brown. Add a splash of hot milk and stir vigorously as the flour and butter mix expands. Continue to add the milk a little at a time, stirring between each addition. Add the wine, then stir in the grated cheese and parsley. Season to taste.
4. Pour the sauce over the fish and top with the mashed potato. Cover with foil and bake for 15 minutes. Remove the foil and cook for a further 20 minutes until the top is golden brown.

RASPBERRY AND WHITE CHOCOLATE SPONGE PUDDINGS

These little individual desserts are proper puddings. They taste wicked and the flavours go together very well indeed. Suzanne gives some of the credit for the recipe to some friends who live in Spain but this is a very British creation. Serve it with some ice cream and you get the wonderful combination of hot and cold in the same mouthful. Suzanne used a delicious local vanilla ice cream made in the Eden valley.

Serves 4

80g white chocolate
1 punnet fresh raspberries
2 medium eggs
2 teaspoons vanilla extract

170g caster sugar
75g self-raising flour
200ml double cream

METHOD

1. Preheat the oven to 180°C/350°F/gas mark 4. Take four large ramekins or mini soufflé dishes, break the white chocolate into small shards and divide among them with the raspberries.
2. To make the spongy topping, using an electric beater mix the eggs, vanilla essence and the sugar. Add the flour and mix well. Add the cream and mix well – you are aiming for a loose batter about the same consistency as a thickish pancake mix.
3. Divide the mixture between the dishes and place in the oven. Look at them after 25 minutes (they will probably need 30); they should look golden when done. Don't worry if you undercook them slightly – the gooey mixture will still be delicious. Serve in their dishes with a ball of good-quality vanilla ice cream melting on top.

DINNER WITH

HEATHER PRITCHETT

OAKHANGER, CHESHIRE

HEATHER AND MICHAEL PRITCHETT live in an elegant house in a very sleek part of Cheshire; it's the sort of countryside that is home to a great many riding stables and well-maintained gardens. The Pritchett's house, Pear Tree Farm, is almost chocolate-box pretty and comes with eight acres of paddocks and gardens, enough room for Michael to justify owning a classic grey Fergie tractor and for Heather to keep Indian runner ducks, Archangel pigeons and guinea fowl.

Strangely, there's not much history of farming at Pear Tree Farm. In recent memory the building was part of the ablutions block belonging to a large sports ground and you can still see the faint outline of a long-gone cricket square in one of the paddocks. There are, however, a great many fruit trees and in the autumn it lives up to its name. Michael is the international sales director of a company that makes medical equipment and Heather is part of a consultancy that specialises in company communications – helping management by auditing current practice and commissioning staff surveys.

Heather is a good cook and every step towards creating the meal is meticulously organised – she sets great store by the old-fashioned concept of a 'cooking plan'. Although largely self-taught she credits some of her interest in cooking to a cousin of Michael's – Stephanie Willis – and it's one of Stephanie's recipes for a double-stuffed, boned-out chicken that is to be the centrepiece of our dinner. Ms Willis inherited her love of cooking from her grandmother who was chef to King Edward VIII. Indeed, Granny taught Stephanie to bone out a chicken and Stephanie taught Heather! Within the family eyes still go misty when the revered 'Edward trifle' is mentioned and if the chicken dish is anything to go by it is probably very good indeed.

One thing that Heather is very firm about is the importance of buying well and working with the seasons, although 'not-buying' would perhaps be a better way of putting it. The Pritchetts are enmeshed in a successful rural barter network – thus a couple of dozen duck eggs or a basket of apples may be transformed into a bag of Cheshire potatoes, or ripe tomatoes, or some epic cucumbers. It all makes perfect sense. For the rest of the shopping list, meat (the magnificent free range chicken) comes from a local butcher and an all-Cheshire cheeseboard comes from an outpost of Williams of Wem – perfectionist cheese specialists.

To start with Heather made a salmon and watercress terrine, a pretty pink and green slice that was teamed with a coarsely chopped raita made with cucumber, yogurt and a splodge of horseradish. That was followed by a pear, pea and spinach soup. This was a revelation: who would have thought that something so simple as leaving the skins on the pears would have such a profound effect on the finished dish? Each emerald green spoonful was a joy – great flavours and a distinctive texture. Then the boned and stuffed chicken, made to a recipe handed down by a circuitous route from the table of Edward VIII. This was served with simply cooked Cheshire potatoes, runner beans and a combination of leeks and carrots that has been sautéed together (a marriage that worked very well), plus a traditional bread sauce (another family recipe) and a strong gravy – nothing over the top, just a smart supermarket stock tweaked into shape. For pudding there was a choice of a notable ruby red jelly, which held suspended various different seasonal fruits, served with cream; or a gooseberry and pistachio crumble. Finally a large board covered with eight local cheeses took centre stage.

For a couple that lists Les Berceaux in Epernay, in the Champagne region of France, as their favourite restaurant, the Pritchetts seem to cook admirably unfussy food. Dishes are underpinned by top quality ingredients and simple flavour combinations. At first glance a boned-out roast chicken with two stuffings sounds like an ambitious and difficult project but it turns out to be relatively easy to accomplish. What a good way to impress at your next dinner party.

SALMON AND WATERCRESS TERRINE

This terrine is deceptively simple to make and looks very good when cut into slices showing a pretty balance of pink and green. Heather dresses each plate with some hard-boiled guinea fowl eggs and serves the dish with a cucumber and yogurt raita on the side. You can either make it in a specialist terrine trough or use a standard loaf tin.

Serves 6

500g sliced smoked salmon	150ml double cream
600g salmon fillet	2 bunches peppery watercress
3 duck eggs (or substitute large hen's eggs)	salt and freshly ground black pepper

METHOD

1. Preheat the oven to 180°C/350°F/gas mark 4. Line your terrine dish (see above) with the sliced smoked salmon, being careful to overlap the joins and leave some hanging over the edge to fold in.
2. Skin the salmon fillet and divide into two. Cut one half into 1cm dice, season with salt and pepper and set aside while you prepare the rest of the filling.
3. Place the remaining salmon, eggs and cream in a food processor and whizz until you have a smooth paste. Add the watercress – use it all except for the thickest main stalks – and whizz some more. Season to taste.
4. Assemble the terrine. Put a layer of the green mixture in the bottom of your smoked salmon-lined dish. Scatter with the pink salmon cubes, then top up with the remaining green mixture. Bang the tin to get rid of air gaps and fold the hanging smoked salmon neatly over the top. Cover the terrine with foil and cook in a water bath (i.e. in a roasting tin with 1–2cm water), in the oven for 35–40 minutes until firm to the touch.
5. Leave to cool, then refrigerate to chill. To serve, turn the terrine out of the tin and cut into slices (run the knife under a hot tap). Allow the slices to come up to room temperature before serving. Serve with a cucumber raita.

CUCUMBER RAITA

This is very easy to make. There's only one thing to watch out for: the cucumber soaks up seasoning and you'll need a generous hand with the salt and pepper.

Serves 6

300g plain Greek-style yogurt
1 tablespoon hot creamed horseradish sauce

1 large cucumber, cut into 5mm cubes
salt and freshly ground black pepper

METHOD

Spoon the yogurt into a bowl and stir in the horseradish and cucumber. Season well with salt and pepper. Chill before serving.

PEAR, PEA AND SPINACH SOUP

This ends up as an elegant dark green soup with an amazing texture – one that reflects that crystalline grittiness that is characteristic of pear skins. The flavour of pears does not dominate the finished article but the texture is very interesting indeed. This soup freezes beautifully and should be served with a swirl of cream in the centre of each bowlful.

Serves 6

30g unsalted butter
1 large onion, finely chopped
500g firm dessert pears, cored, unpeeled and
roughly chopped
250g spinach leaves (use frozen spinach
at a pinch)

350g frozen peas
150ml Tio Pepe – Fino sherry
850ml chicken stock (supermarket stock
or a cube will suffice)
salt and freshly ground black pepper

METHOD

1. Heat the butter in a pan (preferably the big pan you are going to make the soup in) and sweat the onions until they are soft. Add the pears, spinach and peas and stir well.
2. Add the stock, bring to the boil and then turn down and simmer for 15 minutes or so, until all is soft.
3. Add the sherry then transfer to a food processor and whizz until all is smooth – you can also use a hand-held blender. Season bravely with salt and pepper. Set aside and reheat when you are ready to serve.

TWICE-STUFFED BONED CHICKEN

This dish is much less daunting than it sounds. Boning out a chicken is a skill that can be mastered easily; there are several books offering step-by-step directions and if that still seems too tricky there is an even simpler method – ask your butcher to do it for you! When cooked, the stuffed chicken slices across neatly to reveal the pleasant pattern made by the two stuffings. It is also wonderful served cold so it may be wise to double the quantities and do a pair of chickens – whatever the size of your party it will increase the odds on there being some left over.

Serves 6

1 large free range chicken, boned out

For the first stuffing
25ml olive oil
1 large onion, chopped finely
500g sausagemeat
zest of 1 orange
25ml whisky
freshly ground black pepper

For the second stuffing
3 garlic cloves
500g chestnut mushrooms,
finely chopped
a handful of parsley, finely chopped
salt and freshly ground black pepper

METHOD

1. Preheat the oven to 180°C/350°F/gas mark 4. To make the first stuffing, heat the olive oil in a pan and sweat the onion until soft. In a bowl, mix the onions with the sausagemeat, orange zest and whisky. Season with pepper (the sausagemeat will be salty enough) and set aside.

2. To make the second stuffing, pop the garlic cloves into boiling water and cook for 5–8 minutes until soft, then mash thoroughly. Mix this with the mushrooms and parsley and season with salt and pepper. Set aside.

3. Spread the boned chicken on a board, skin side down. Cover with a layer of the sausage meat stuffing, then arrange the mushroom stuffing in the centre. Bring the chicken together so that it makes a rough cylinder around the two stuffings with the dark mushroom stuffing at the very middle. Sew up the bird to preserve its shape.

4. Place on a trivet, cover with foil and place in the oven. It will take longer to roast than an ordinary chicken because it is solid – about 2 hours – check with a sharp knife after 90 minutes. For the last 30 minutes take the foil off to brown the breast. Rest the bird for 30 minutes before carving.

PEAR TREE FARM JELLY

Who can refuse jelly and cream? This is a rather grown-up jelly, and although not rigorously seasonal, it looks exotic and elegant. You'll need a two-pint jelly mould, although a similar-sized tin bowl will do. Run it under the hot tap, ever so briefly, to turn the jelly out.

Serves 6

2 packets lemon jelly
1 tablespoon redcurrant jelly
50ml framboise de Bourgogne (that's the dark sticky one, the raspberry equivalent of crème de cassis)

fresh fruit as required and available, e.g. plums (stoned), brambles, redcurrants or raspberries from the freezer
double cream, to serve

METHOD

1. Make up the two packets of jelly in a big jug – use only three quarters of the recommended amount of water. Stir in the redcurrant jelly and the framboise. Pour a little jelly into the bottom of the mould, and refrigerate until set. Put to one side and keep warm.
2. Sprinkle the redcurrants and brambles onto the surface, add a little more jelly, and refrigerate until set.
3. Arrange the plum halves on top, cover with the remaining jelly and refrigerate until set. This procedure should ensure that the fruit is suspended in layers. Serve with double cream.

LUNCH WITH
GLENDA JARMAN JONES
LLANIDLOES, POWYS

GLENDA JARMAN JONES lives with her husband Peter in a tidy little house that is tucked into the hillside on the fringes of Llanidloes. The garden is terraced and frames a beautiful view across the valley. When you pitch up for lunch the first drink provides evidence of Glenda's current obsession – it's a sweet and floral elderflower champagne which is poured from a rather incongruous and dusty two-litre fizzy drink bottle.

As well as the very refreshing champagne she has made elderflower cordial – the foundation of her elderflower ice cream – and elderflower and gooseberry jam. As each season comes round Glenda will be out scrumping everything from crab apples to mushrooms or blackberries. There is an air of competence and iron determination about Mrs Jcarman Jones, exactly what you would expect from someone whose CV includes time spent as Ward Sister.

Occasionally you meet people who cook slavishly from recipe books (you know the kind of thing: if the author says 25ml, 26 or 24 won't do); Glenda takes the opposite view – when she cooks she changes the ingredients and challenges the methods and the timing as she goes along. You would suspect that such a cavalier approach would end up with the occasional 'car crash' dish, but for our lunch everything went swimmingly.

Glenda comes from a farming background and she clearly remembers the annual 'pig killing' day, if only because a helpful farm worker would blow up and knot the pig's bladder and it would be given to the children to use as a football! Another consequence of early days on a hill farm is an aversion to lamb and to this day – none of the family will eat lamb.

The lunch menu was a simple one, although the dishes could never be called obvious – a tomato and herb soup (heavily laced with fresh herbs from the garden but with an ever-changing combination depending on whim, as Glenda confesses, 'I'm a fiddler') was served with a strange but beguiling nasturtium relish and home-made bread rolls. The bread rolls were very good indeed – floury, soft and with a well-developed crumb, neither fluffy and white nor wholemeal and leaden but somewhere between the two. The shocking surprise lies in the method part of this recipe – Glenda pops the rolls into a cold oven and then turns it on to heat up gently – most other cooks start by proving the rolls and then put them into a preheated oven.

The main course was a marinated piece of local pork wrapped in bacon and roasted, the accompanying fruit sauce being made with mango. Dessert was a stellar crumble made with local whinberries and served with elderflower ice cream. I'm afraid to say that however hard I tried I was unable to get Mrs Jarman Jones to divulge the recipe for her elderflower ice cream. It went like this: I would enquire politely about the ingredients or techniques and then she would change the subject. Good manners dictate that when you have been stonewalled a few times by a steely-eyed ex-ward sister you give up and move on!

In this case we moved on to an all-Welsh cheeseboard: Perl Las (an elegant blue cheese), Cenarth Brie (rich, yellow and creamy, and certainly the equal of its French ancestor), and the new Llangloffan Blue (this is a rich orange cheese reminiscent of Blacksticks Blue), good to eat but let down by rather uneven blueing. To go with the cheese course the Jarman Joneses produced a formidable array of home-made liqueurs – damson gin, damson port and a stunning blackberry vodka – take heart, I did manage to secure the recipe for that!

SIMPLE BREAD ROLLS

There is something counter-intuitive about putting bread into a cold oven to bake. We are all accustomed to heating the oven before use. Glenda's method is suspiciously simple, but do not fear, it does work; her bread rolls end up well risen with a good texture and an admirable soft outer crust. She uses the excellent artisan flours from Bacheldre Watermill.

Makes 12 rolls

650g strong white flour	80g hard vegetable margarine
650g wholemeal flour	3 tablespoons olive oil
1 tablespoon dried yeast	1 dessertspoon salt
1 tablespoon caster sugar	850ml tepid water

METHOD

1. Put the flour, dried yeast, sugar, margarine, olive oil and salt into the bowl of a food processor. Use the dough hook and set it running as you add the water. Mix for 2 or 3 minutes until you have an even-textured dough.
2. Line an oven sheet with some baking parchment. Form the dough into a dozen rolls and arrange on the parchment. Set aside to prove – they should double in size – for about 45 minutes.
3. Put the rolls into a cold oven. Turn the oven on, set it at 200°C/400°F/gas mark 6 (use the fan if you have one). Check the rolls after 20 minutes, they will probably be done although precise timings vary from oven to oven. To be absolutely sure break a roll open and check.

NASTURTIUM RELISH

Glenda served this green, crunchy, nutty, peppery-tasting relish with the tomato soup; it worked very well as a contrasting taste and texture but was equally delicious on a buttered bread roll. It is probably best made as and when required although you could develop a version that preserves the nasturtiums and has a longer shelf life. Surprisingly good. Nasturtium seeds are often used as a caper substitute, and while this relish is best made with fresh seeds from your own flowers, you could use pickled or salted capers instead, but do make sure you rinse them thoroughly.

Fills a 150ml jar

2 handfuls of fresh nasturtium seeds
50g sesame seeds
1 dessertspoon extra virgin olive oil
1 dessertspoon balsamic vinegar

1 teaspoon toasted sesame oil
coarse sea salt and
freshly ground black pepper

METHOD

Roughly chop the nasturtium seeds , then mix well with the sesame seeds, olive oil, balsamic vinegar and sesame oil. Season lavishly with the salt and pepper and mix well.

TOMATO AND HERB SOUP

This simple tomato soup has an unexpected depth of flavour. It is important not to be too thorough when liquidising as a roughish texture is desirable. The natural acidity of the tomatoes is helped along by the oranges.

Serves 4

25g unsalted butter
25ml olive oil
2 red onions, peeled and finely sliced
2 leeks, finely chopped
2 carrots, peeled and finely sliced
1 garlic clove, finely chopped
500g tomatoes, skinned and thoroughly chopped

2 large oranges, peeled and thoroughly chopped
bunch of fresh mixed herbs (use any or all of: garlic chives, oregano, rosemary, lemon balm, mint leaves and sage), finely chopped
1.5 litres chicken stock (you can use supermarket stock)
salt and freshly ground black pepper

METHOD

1. Melt the butter and olive oil together in a deep frying pan, add the onions, leeks, carrots and garlic and soften over a low heat.
2. Transfer the contents of the frying pan to a large pan. Add the tomatoes and orange, then the herbs and the stock. Bring to the boil and then turn down and simmer gently for 30 minutes.
3. Liquidise with a hand-held blender. Be careful not to overdo it, as some texture is good for the final soup. Season with salt and pepper. Serve with bread rolls and nasturtium relish.

MARINATED PORK WITH MANGO SAUCE

Pork tenderloin is a difficult cut to cook well. It is bereft of the fat so important for lubrication and needs help in the flavour department. Glenda gets her pork from a local supplier – Jamie Ward – and lavishes care and attention on its preparation. The fruitiness of the sauce works well with the meat. Serve this with simply cooked fresh vegetables – new potatoes and green beans work well.

Serves 4

1 bunch of mixed herbs, e.g. thyme, sage, lemon balm, oregano
25ml olive oil
3 lemons
2 whole pork tenderloins
6 rashers of dry-cured streaky bacon
freshly ground black pepper
50ml dry Martini

For the mango sauce
25g unsalted butter
1 large onion, peeled and very finely diced
1 clove garlic, crushed
1 ripe mango
2 dessert apples
1 glass dry white wine
salt and freshly ground black pepper
150g crème fraîche

METHOD

1. Put the herbs, olive oil and the juice of one of the lemons into a liquidiser and whizz them up until you have a fine paste.
2. Take the tenderloins and cut regular slashes, about 1cm deep, on an angle. Rub the herb paste into them. Cut the remaining lemons into wedges and press them into the cuts. Leave to marinate in the fridge for a minimum of 2 hours and maximum of 24 hours.
3. To cook, preheat the oven to 180°C/350°F/gas mark 4. Take the bacon rashers and 'spread' them out on a board with the back of a knife. Season each tenderloin with black pepper, and wrap the meat in bacon. Then wrap the pork rolls in clingfilm and splash in the Martini just before you seal up the parcel.
4. Cook in the oven for 30 minutes: test with a skewer – the meat is done when it is barely pink inside. Remove the clingfilm and cut into elegant slices.
5. Meanwhile, make the mango sauce. Melt the butter in a frying pan and cook the onions and garlic gently until soft.

6. Peel the mango and put the flesh into a liquidiser. Peel and core the apples and add the flesh to the liquidiser. Whizz until smooth. Add this to the onions and garlic and cook the mixture gently to blend the flavours.
7. Stir in the white wine and season with salt and pepper. Before serving, stir in the crème fraîche and warm through, being careful not to let it boil. Serve with the pork.

WHINBERRY CRUMBLE

Whinberries are small native blueberries – Glenda picks hers in the Hafren Forest, which is close to Llanidloes. They are also known as whortleberries in the West Country and blaeberries in Scotland – supermarket blueberries make a practical substitute but lack the intensity and sweetness of the wild fruit. Adding a crumbled Weetabix to the mixture will help the texture – it's a great 'secret ingredient'. Glenda serves this crumble with her home-made elderflower ice cream but stubbornly refuses to share that recipe! Thankfully thick cream also works remarkably well.

Serves 4

500g whinberries
180g muscovado sugar
120g unsalted butter

180g plain white flour
1 Weetabix

METHOD

1. Preheat the oven to 180°C/350°F/gas mark 4. Put the berries into an appropriately sized pie dish.
2. Rub the sugar, butter, flour and Weetabix together until the texture resembles breadcrumbs then sprinkle over the berries – do not press it down too firmly. Bake for 30–40 minutes until the top is crisp and golden. Allow to cool before serving.

BLACKBERRY VODKA

Glenda specialises in home-made drinks including this charming blackberry vodka. You have to be careful not to overdo the sugar. Use a Kilner jar or any other jar with a wide neck that can be completely sealed.

Fills a 1 litre jar

A good picking of wild blackberries   100g white sugar per bottle of vodka
1 vanilla pod   1 bottle of full strength vodka

METHOD

1. Lightly crush the blackberries and put them in the jar (it needs to be about 70 per cent full). Split the vanilla pod and spear it into the heart of the blackberries. Add the sugar and top up with the vodka. Seal the jar and keep in a dark place for at least 6 months, giving it a shake every now and then. If the level drops as it settles, top up with some more vodka.
2. Strain and either bottle or drink!

DINNER WITH
HAYLEY CRIPPS
KING'S NORTON, BIRMINGHAM

DESPITE IT BEING THE NEAREST large city to my current home I am
shockingly unfamiliar with Birmingham. I know about the Wrottesley Street
end of Chinatown and I have raided the so-called Balti Triangle with its unique
approach to curry, but the rest of Brum is pretty much uncharted territory. In
Worcestershire Brummies are known rather disparagingly as 'yam yams', a
moniker that allegedly derives from the epithet 'y'am alright y'am', which can be
translated as 'You are alright my good fellow, you are.' None of which background
was much help as I drove into Kings Norton to have dinner with Hayley Cripps.

Hayley lives (with her husband and a rambunctious puppy called Louie) in a small,
immaculately-kept terraced house on a modern estate. Driving there is a good idea,
partly because there is no other transport – except a bus every couple of hours –
and partly because you get some kind of grasp of the enormous size of these
sprawling housing estates, as each one merges into the next. Lots of houses and
blocks of flats, all neat and orderly, but there's a remarkable shortage of pubs,
shops and restaurants.

During the week Hayley teaches IT and business studies at a local school and she certainly has that cheerful and non-nonsense way with her, the kind of presence you need to quell a room of boisterous children. She is also a talented and ambitious cook. Her dinner party menu shows that she is not afraid to experiment (halloumi and rocket salad), she marries flavours together well (duck breast on Savoy cabbage with bacon) and she is quite unfazed by complex cheffy desserts requiring pinpoint timing (chocolate Vesuvius pudding).

Hayley's love for cooking came via her grandmother. 'My mum worked very long hours and it fell to my Grandmother to put our meals on the table,' she says. 'She was a very good baker but also someone who realised that while a love of cooking is important, the 'family meal' is an even more important concept. She was most particular about the formalities – including setting the table.' There's no doubt that Hayley has been influenced by the telly chefs, although she is adamant that while she may watch Gordon Ramsay 'for entertainment' she never picks up on any of his recipes. She also talks warmly about Raymond Blanc and his show *The Restaurant* and admires the way he can be single-minded about sourcing ingredients. The bitter truth is that for Hayley and everyone else living in the outskirts of Birmingham, shopping is the continuing problem. 'For the dinner tonight I have had to get everything from a single supermarket. It would be different if we lived somewhere like Bourneville, where they have shops selling organic vegetables, a traditional butcher and a proper baker, but for us that sort of shopping is an indulgence and a luxury.'

It would be very chastening for all those food writers who are incessantly banging on about shopping frequently for fresh food; about eating seasonally; about organic vegetables and about simple dishes to see how the rubric works when lack of time and a fixed budget mean that you have to do all your shopping in one hit at a single supermarket. As Hayley puts it, 'To be a really good cook you have to have more time and slightly more money.' I would disagree. I think Hayley is a really good cook, and the fact that she manages to cook so well without access to really good shops is even more impressive. Her dishes are sophisticated and satisfying, you get strong flavours and attractive-looking platefuls. Hayley has a good palate, a confident attitude and she thinks about what she is doing. It does make you wonder what effect giving the big supermarkets control over what there is to buy and what we must pay for it has on our nation. Good shopping is the precursor of good cooking and having a choice is fundamental to good shopping. When it comes to food the choice here is severely limited; won't that inevitably reduce the number of good cooks in this part of Birmingham? That would be a shame. Here are the recipes Hayley cooked, and very delicious they are too.

HALLOUMI AND ROCKET SALAD

This is a jolly little 'starter salad' that delivers both a satisfying mix of flavours and combination of textures. Everything you need is easily sourced at the supermarket and due to the extended season of rocket this salad can provide a much-needed glimpse of greenery even in the depths of winter. Be careful when seasoning the dressing as halloumi is a brined cheese and can prove salty. If you prefer, this salad works just as well when you substitute watercress for the rocket.

Serves 4

150ml good, but not great, olive oil
75ml good, but not great, balsamic vinegar
2 teaspoons wholegrain mustard
salt and freshly ground black pepper
50g sun-dried tomatoes in oil (reserve 2 teaspoons of the oil)

50g pine nuts
1 pack halloumi cheese, cut into eight 1cm slices
2 bags wild rocket leaves
crusty bread, to serve

METHOD

1. Start by making the dressing. Put the oil, vinegar and mustard in a jar with a tight-fitting lid. Add the 2 teaspoons oil from the sun-dried tomatoes, a pinch of salt and a few twists of black pepper. Seal and shake like mad. Taste and adjust the seasoning. Set aside.
2. Toast the pine nuts in a dry frying pan – you want them browned but not blackened. Chop the sun-dried tomatoes into manageable strips and set aside.
3. Heat a pan to cook the halloumi (a ridged grill pan is ideal but any heavy frying pan will do). Fry until the outside of the cheese is sealed – a ridged pan will leave pretty 'grill marks'.
4. In a large bowl, mix the rocket and sun-dried tomatoes. Shake the dressing and add, tossing so that every leaf is coated.
5. Put a mound of leaves in the centre of each plate, add a couple of slices of halloumi and a sprinkle of pine nuts. Serve with crusty bread.

DUCK BREASTS WITH SAVOY CABBAGE AND BACON

Savoy cabbage is one of the great joys of autumn – wrinkly, dark green and with a nutty sweet taste. But such is our obsession with meat that serving up a dish of just cabbage would probably leave your guests feeling rather short-changed. This dish solves that problem by topping the pile of cabbage on offer with a meaty duck breast, and the taste of smoky bacon cabbage works very well with the juiciness of the duck.

Serves 4

a tiny splash of olive oil	1 medium Savoy cabbage, finely shredded
8 rashers smoked streaky bacon	salt and freshly ground black pepper
1 red onion, finely chopped	4 duck breasts

METHOD

1. Preheat the oven to 200°C/400°F/gas mark 6. Put a smear of olive oil into a deep casserole dish (with a lid), put it on the hob and bring up the heat. (You are aiming somewhere between stir-frying and braising. The bacon and onion need frying to bring out their flavour, the cabbage needs 'steaming' to make it tender.) Cut the bacon rashers into postage stamp sized pieces and sizzle in the pot. When the bacon releases its fat add the onions and cook until softened.

2. Add the cabbage and stir everything together. After five minutes, when the cabbage starts to wilt, season with freshly ground black pepper. Pop the lid on and turn off the heat. Leave for at least 5 minutes, while you attend to the duck.

3. Put a pan on the hob to heat up – preferably a pan that you can transfer to the oven. Your aim is to seal the meat on the hob and then cook it through in the oven. Pat the duck breasts dry with kitchen towel and season well with salt and pepper. Press the skin side down in the hot pan and cook for 2 minutes, then turn over and seal the 'meaty' side for 2 minutes.

4. Transfer to the oven (skin side up) and roast for about 10 minutes, more or less depending on how pink you like your duck. When you're wondering if the meat is done nothing beats cutting into it with a knife and seeing what's what! When the duck is cooked let it rest for 5 minutes in a warm place.

5. To serve, mound the cabbage in the centre of the plate, being careful not to miss the juices. Cut the duck breasts across into neat slices and arrange on top of the cabbage. Serve with a plain potato dish – 'crushed' small potatoes works well.

CHOCOLATE VESUVIUS PUDDINGS

This kind of 'runny inside, cakey outside' fondant pud used to be the preserve of chefs. And the first recipes were difficult as they involved refrigerating a core so that it could withstand the heat of the oven and go on to become the delicious chocolate lava bit when the pud was cut into. These puds play to everyone's weak spot – chocolate – and delivers a good belt of flavour without being over-sweet. The mechanism used to achieve the liquid centre is a simple one: you cook the pud for the precise length of time it takes to firm up the outside, but not long enough to do anything more than heat up the interior goo. Judging this precisely may take practice, so a trial run is recommended before unleashing them on a smart dinner party.

Serves 4

200g dark chocolate, 70% cocoa solids	3 large eggs
50g unsalted butter, softened	30g plain flour
50g soft brown sugar	1 tablespoon cocoa powder

METHOD

1. Butter four individual ramekins. Melt the chocolate (the flashy way is to pop it in the microwave but beware – with just a second or two's inattention it can easily spoil; the steady way is to break the chocolate up and melt it in a bowl set over simmering water, taking care not to let the bowl touch the water).
2. Take a whisk and cream the butter with the sugar in a mixing bowl. Beat in the eggs, then stir in the flour and cocoa powder, and finally the melted chocolate – you're aiming for a smooth batter. Alternatively you could put everything into a food processor and whizz.
3. Fill the ramekins and bake for about 10 minutes – the puds are ready when they have risen and firmed. The outside will look 'cakey'. Just how long they should cook for will depend on your oven, but after a trial run you'll find that judging this is much easier than it sounds. Turn out the puds and serve with cream.

THE BIG CHEESE

GLOUCESTERSHIRE

PICTURE THE SCENE IN THE LARGE HALL at the Duke of York Barracks in Chelsea where, at 9am sharp on 23 September 1999, I was lining up with forty or so food writers, cheese makers, cheese graders and cheese retailers: we had put on our white coats, polished our cheese-irons and picked up our clipboards and pencils. The room fell silent as Juliet Harbutt stood on a chair to welcome us as judges of the sixth British Cheese Awards and to brief us on our responsibilities. Catching sight of some movement at the back of the hall Juliet paused. 'Why are you late?' she boomed in a voice so loud that it would have gladdened the heart of the Regimental Sergeant Major on the parade ground outside. The latecomer – food editor of one of the serious Sunday papers and a rather dapper, urbane fellow – mumbled his apologies, while Juliet proceeded to tear him off a strip on the importance of punctuality and good manners. It was like being transported back to the schoolroom and the assembled hacks (grateful that they had arrived on time and that someone else had copped the flak) almost dared to snigger. But you don't snigger when Juliet is telling you something, a sense of self-preservation sees to that.

Juliet Harbutt is a determined woman and someone for whom the description 'feisty' fits like a glove. Over fifteen years she has done an enormous amount for British cheese – at the first British Cheese Awards in 1994, ninety-seven producers entered 296 different cheeses, while in 2009, 189 producers entered 884 cheeses. All of which is all the more remarkable as this champion of British cheese is a foreigner. When asked to recall her first taste of cheese she talks ruefully of Chesdale, which is the New Zealand equivalent of a Dairylea cheese triangle.

But Juliet was always driven by a love of cheese, so much so that a matter of months after setting up a small restaurant and deli in New Zealand she set off on a trip to Europe to do a cooking course in Paris and hone her skills as a cook. This was one of those gentle 'finishing school' operations where the hidden agenda was to allow well-heeled young American women a few months' cavorting in Paris. But the course did take gastronomy seriously and no less an expert than Steven Spurrier would accompany the students on trips to visit wine merchants, the Poilâne bakery and the famous cheese shop Androuët. 'I tasted those cheeses and my life changed. It was as simple as that.' Juliet was bowled over.

They say that we all have at least one life-changing idea during our lifetime but only a tiny percentage of us recognise the moment and are quick enough to do anything about it. Juliet Harbutt seized her opportunity with both hands, hurtled back to New Zealand, sold her deli and returned to London hell-bent on opening a proper cheese shop. 'In the 1980s cheese shops were few and far between, and the number of places doing the job properly made a very short list indeed.' From this crucible came a seminal cheese and wine retailer called Jeroboams that endures today. For once someone was taking cheese seriously and for once excellence was the watchword rather than lip service.

Although her love of cheese started with the great French cheeses, pretty soon Juliet realised that there was a fledgling British cheese industry that was badly in need of a champion. The advent of milk quotas had meant that lots of farmers were looking to cheese-making as a way of diversifying, and the number of new cheeses being invented each year was rising steadily, but the British cheeses were always seen as second best. Juliet, however, was from New Zealand, where they have a different idea of what is and is not possible. She approached a major supermarket, and helped them set up a training programme so that their staff could tell their Cheddar from their Stilton, then she persuaded the supermarket to sponsor a new competition called the British Cheese Awards. The structure of these awards was masterly, and very helpful to the cheese-makers, as every entrant got feedback whether or not they won a medal. If a cheese was too bland, too salty or too chalky, now the cheese-maker could get an impartial view of what had gone wrong. The way the judging was set up was also subtly media-savvy: teams of three would include a knowledgeable cheese technician, a retailer and a food writer. It seems obvious now, but many of these food writers (myself included) became lifelong fans of British cheese and all of them went away and wrote about the wondrous new cheeses they had tried. Juliet Harbutt is a dab hand at self-fulfilling prophecies.

In 1996 the French (who with typical Gallic assurance find it hard to concede that anyone else knows anything about cheese) invited Britain to send some cheeses to Besançon University where they were attempting to create the world's largest cheeseboard and so claim a place in the *Guinness Book of Records*. The organisers set up a small table in a corner and awaited the arrival of Le Stilton, Le Cheddar and perhaps Le Wensleydale. But Les Brits packed an array of cheeses into several large boxes and sent them off via a courier. When the UK delegation, headed by Juliet, arrived in Besançon a nervous and defensive French official claimed that all 296 British entries had been lost en route. Juliet would have none of it and conducted a thorough search of the cold store, only to find that Britain's cheeses had inexplicably become hidden at the back under some boxes. The French capitulated and had to live with the unpalatable truth that Britain provided nearly a third of the cheeses for their record-breaking 'World's Largest Cheeseboard'.

There's a saying among cheese makers that while it's easy enough to make a cheese it's very tricky to make a great one, and more difficult than that to turn out something that is consistently excellent month in, month out. Cheese-makers know that they are only as good as the cheese they made yesterday – it's a straightforward process but one with many variables: the temperature, the humidity, the barometric pressure, even a cheese-maker with a hangover can influence the final product. Juliet's view is that the most important attribute of any cheese-maker is a good sense of humour and cites Father Patrice at the Abbaye de Tamié near Lake Annecy in the Savoie. Tamié is a magnificent cow's milk cheese, which is sold wrapped in blue paper bearing the white cross of Malta. It is made by Trappist monks and somehow they have to combine the gentle, unhurried cheese-making process with breaking off seven times a day to pray. Father Patrice admits that sometimes his prayers contain an extraneous and practical request like 'Please curdle properly'. There is a definite link between a calm attitude and good cheese and Juliet points to another example closer to home. The Loch Arthur Community in south-west Scotland was established in 1984 for vulnerable men and women with learning disabilities and they make a consistently good cheese. As Juliet stresses, 'Safe and steady gets it done. This is a job that requires endless patience. Cheese waits for no man and can be hurried by no man!'

Over the past fifteen years the British Cheese Awards has given out thousands of medals and helped scores of fledgling producers market their first cheeses. It has also seen its fair share of oddities. Cheese-makers are an eccentric bunch and are not above a little strategic skulduggery. Some have been known to make special cheeses for the competition, while others let them age a little bit longer – often a cheese entered in a class as eight weeks old will have a true age nearer to sixteen weeks. And then there are the bizarre added flavours – no one who tasted it could ever forget the cheese with coffee (this shocker was made with, and rolled in, coffee grounds!). Or how about a new Cheddar shot through with chocolate chips? In some ways we should be grateful that such experiments push the boundaries, just so long as they don't become the 'next big thing'.

After a lifetime as a cheese-oholic, and given all the work she has done as a marketing consultant to both the retail trade and the big creameries, it is somewhat surprising that it was the new Millennium before Juliet ended up developing her own cheeses. The opportunity arose when a young gentleman farmer moved to the Cotswolds: her new neighbour was ex-Blur bass guitarist Alex James and he is almost as keen on cheese as she is. 'I've always loved cheese and when we toured Japan diehard fans would throw cheese at me when we were on stage. It sounds OK until you realise that nearly all cheese in Japan comes in tins!' Together Juliet and Alex founded the Evenlode Partnership and produced a series of new cheeses, including Little Wallop, a goat's cheese washed in cider brandy and then wrapped in vine leaves; Farleigh Wallop, a soft goat's cheese, and Blue Monday, a rich cow's milk blue.

Much has been written about the 'rights' and 'wrongs' of food and wine matching, and it is often cheese and wine combinations that come in for particularly close scrutiny. Juliet maintains an open mind on the subject, but starts from a cheese lover's standpoint. 'Cheese is every bit as varied as fruit or meat and it would be impossible to issue a sweeping edict that all meat is best eaten with such and such a wine.' Thank goodness we have moved on from the days when a snooty head waiter would shudder and sigh if you had the temerity to order red wine with fish. Juliet's point is more broadly based and she sees a good match between various cheeses and different drinks: traditional hard cheeses go well with beer; soft cheeses are a good match with cider; blue cheeses work with something sweeter; smellier cheeses cry out for rich red wine. But more interestingly she appropriates the French idea of terroir and recommends trying local drinks with local cheeses. We live in an age where the limitations on what can be grown where are changing (a grove of olive trees has been planted near Oxford, for example), but look back over a thousand years and you'll find traditional partnerships and these often are as successful today as they have always been: West Country cider and West Country Cheddars; crumbly Wensleydale and Yorkshire ales – perhaps in the future new British cheeses will sit easily with elegant English white wines.

In 1986 an Italian journalist called Carlo Petrini was so horrified when he saw a garish McDonalds fast food restaurant by the famous Spanish Steps in Rome that he started the Slow Food movement. As the world was being flooded by fast food, he reckoned it was time to stand up for the opposite position – Slow Food. This movement was concerned that food should be pleasurable; that it should be wholesome; that it should be eco-friendly; and that it should have a pronounced local character. It's no surprise that Juliet Harbutt established one of the first Slow Food convivia in Britain and meets with the forty or so members of the Cotswold Slow Food Convivium several times a year, as well as leading the British delegation to the famous biennial cheese show held in Bra, Italy.

It's often the case that cheese ends up being the grace note at the end of a meal rather than the centrepiece of the festivities. And it's true that very few farmers depend solely on cheese to make a living. But once you are bitten with the cheese bug you'll find that cheese is an increasingly versatile and downright delicious food, and you'll probably want to raise a glass to pioneers like Juliet Harbutt.

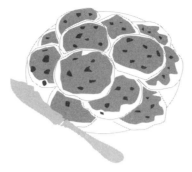

AFTERNOON TEA WITH
BARBARA ATKINS
PEMBRIDGE, HEREFORDSHIRE

PEMBRIDGE is one of those implausibly pretty 'black and white' Herefordshire villages. It has everything from a small stream, green fields and cider apple orchards to village shops and a couple of thriving pubs. It hangs like a large bead on the twisty, turning main road – this county is a telling reminder of how things used to be before there were motorways or even dual carriageways; journeys that appear short on the map take a long while to accomplish and a succession of tractors burbling through the lanes force drivers to slow down and enjoy the scenery.

Barbara Atkins is one of those beady-eyed ladies of a certain age and her bookshelves contain everything from Jamie Oliver to William Hague's biography of William Pitt the Younger. In the 1960s she made a living as sales assistant at a tractor dealership, writing out the paperwork for gruff farmers more used to spitting on a handshake as they bought their first little grey Ferguson. Barbara has raised a slew of children – all of them bright and with a high proportion of talented musicians among their ranks – and her cooking style has been tempered by a commitment to family meal times. Although she didn't learn to cook as a child she has proud memories of her mother cooking pies on large round tin trays borrowed from the local pub – it was the only way to get a pie big enough to feed the seven hungry children. She is also nostalgic about 'proper chips' cooked in home-rendered beef dripping.

Somehow Barbara and her husband Hayden have preserved the idea of afternoon tea long after the children have left to take care of their own families. This is a household where, as she says, 'We've always had puddings and we've always had tea. One feels deprived without a bit of cake in the tin.'

How did we allow the comfortable pleasures of home-baking to become a forgotten art? When you make a cake for yourself there are so many advantages – you know that it will be fresh; you know exactly what goes into it; furthermore, you can tailor the cake to suit yourself – leave out the currants, add some glacé ginger. While commercially made cakes and biscuits can show a heavy hand with the additives and preservatives you don't have to follow suit at home. There can also be price advantages – home-made cakes often work out cheaper, although factory biscuits almost always undercut home made.

What is interesting about Barbara's recipes is how basic they are. Yes, some core skills are required, but generally if you follow the simple method these recipes will work. Modern interpretations of classic home-baking recipes so often leave much to chance – I am thinking of the 'put everything into the food processor' school of cake mixing. Old-fashioned techniques like sifting the flour to get air into it, creaming the fat with the sugar and beating the eggs before adding them help the alchemy that is a good cake and are not that difficult to master. For some recipes Barbara also uses block margarine, not the mimsy, spreadable, vegetable stuff or even butter – but hard block margarine – she is convinced that it makes better biscuits. Her peanut biscuits are magnificent, crisp and rich – like those superior and high-priced 'cookies' you find on supermarket shelves. For the boiled fruit cake and the Welsh cakes, however, you should use butter.

Sitting in a pretty kitchen in Pembridge with a cup of strong tea and plates laden with Welsh cakes, slices of fruit cake, crisp peanut biscuits and ridiculously smooth fudge it's hard to understand why such delights should be rarities rather than daily fare. Granted most of us are busy working when the clock strikes tea-time, but these splendidly self-indulgent treats should not be allowed to die out. Try the recipes; they are not difficult. Enjoy the fruits of your labours warm from the oven – they will be delicious.

BOILED FRUIT CAKE

This is a very delicious rich fruit cake that ends up exceedingly moist, almost juicy. The secret lies in pre-cooking the fruit with the butter and sugar. Baking the cake in a bread tin also protects the interior of the cake (leaving it moist) while still allowing the surface of the cake to crisp nicely. As a bonus you get a practical, simple slice rather than the usual wedge. Barbara Atkins attributes this cake to a recipe passed on by the vicar's wife in the village of Canon Pyon.

Serves 8

110g butter
175g light brown sugar
350g mixed dried fruit
200g tin pineapple pieces, partially drained

175g glacé cherries, halved
2 large eggs, beaten
225g self-raising flour

METHOD

1. Preheat the oven to 180°F/350°C/gas mark 4. Grease and line an old-fashioned rectangular 900g loaf tin with baking parchment.
2. Place the butter, sugar, mixed dried fruit, pineapple and half the juice in a pan. Heat gently, then turn down the heat and cook for 5 minutes, stirring continuously to avoid sticking. Remove from the heat and leave to cool for about 90 minutes. Do not be tempted to continue until the mix is cool, as this standing time will allow the fruit to soak up all the juices and plump up.
3. Transfer to a large bowl and add the cherries, mixing well. Then add the eggs and beat in. Finally stir in the flour until you have an even batter. Pour into the prepared tin and bake for 1 hour 15 minutes. After an hour, test by inserting a slender needle to the heart of the cake, when cooked the needle will remain 'clean'. Then give the cake a further 5 minutes for safety's sake! This cake can sink disappointingly in the middle, but an extra 5 minutes' cooking time will save you from this fate.

WELSH CAKES

This Welsh cake recipe came to Barbara Atkins via a nanny who moved to Herefordshire from Carmarthen. There's a lot of argument about just what differentiates Welsh cakes and scones but, broadly speaking, Welsh cakes tend to be made with butter and eggs while scone recipes are simpler and tend to favour margarine and milk. Barbara's Welsh cakes are very good indeed; they have a good crust and a fluffy interior and need little more adornment than a dab of butter.

Makes about 20

450g self-raising flour	110g currants
1 teaspoon salt	2 large eggs, beaten
225g butter, plus extra for greasing	a little milk
110g caster sugar	

METHOD

1. The first thing to attend to is your griddle. This could be a flat-iron griddle, a baking stone or even a heavy-based frying pan. The rule of thumb is that the cooking surface will work better a little too cool than it will when a little too hot. Lick your forefinger and touch the griddle: it should feel hot but not unbearably so. It is also important to practise and be prepared to throw it away if it doesn't work. The griddle should have the merest smear of butter to prevent sticking.
2. Sift the flour and salt into a mixing bowl. Cut the butter into cubes, and rub it into the flour until the mixture resembles breadcrumbs. Stir in the sugar and currants. Work in the beaten egg and just enough milk to bring the mixture together. You are aiming for the same consistency as shortcrust pastry.
3. Flour a board or tabletop and roll out the dough until it is about 5mm thick. (There are different schools of thought when it comes to Welsh cakes : some people like them thin and some prefer them thicker. Be prepared to experiment.)
4. Cook the cakes on the lightly greased griddle for about 3 minutes a side – you are aiming for a golden colour outside and a completely cooked interior. Transfer to a wire rack and leave to cool.
5. There are two ways to enjoy the perfect Welsh cake – they are always better warm – you can have them plain with a dusting of caster sugar or popped under the grill with a dab of butter.

PEANUT BISCUITS

We have all become rather lazy. And we have all become accustomed to shop-bought biscuits. Try this simple and practical recipe for peanut biscuits once and you will be hooked; they are improbably crisp and surprisingly delicious. The secret lies in the counterpoint between the salted peanuts and the sweeter ingredients. As to the provenance of these biscuits, Barbara Atkins can remember making them in the 1960s but cannot be certain where the recipe originated.

Makes about 12

110g 'block' baking margarine
220g caster sugar
1 large egg, beaten
90g self-raising flour
$^1/_2$ teaspoon baking powder

$^1/_2$ teaspoon bicarbonate of soda
75g porridge oats
75g cornflakes, crushed
100g roasted salted peanuts

METHOD

1. Preheat the oven to 160°C/325°F/gas mark 3. Line a baking sheet with silicone baking parchment.
2. In a large mixing bowl, cream the margarine and sugar until very light and fluffy. Add the beaten egg and mix well. Sift in the flour, baking powder and bicarbonate of soda. Stir in the oats, cornflakes and peanuts and mix thoroughly.
3. Place small piles of the mixture on the parchment (each spoonful should be about the size of a small plum). Space them out carefully as they spread a great deal during cooking. Bake for 10–12 minutes; keep an eye on the biscuits and be sure to take them out before they darken. Transfer to a wire rack to cool and store in an airtight container.

FUDGE

There are hundreds of recipes for fudge and north of the border the Scots have hundreds of recipes for tablet. Some people love tablet and loathe fudge and vice versa. Getting any fudge or tablet recipe to work is very vexing; everything sounds so simple up until the moment when you try to replicate it in your own kitchen. Making good fudge is a triumph of technique over ingredients. What makes Barbara's fudge so unusual is this: if you follow the recipe and the method carefully you will succeed. Your reward will be a pale, unctuous, melt-in-the mouth dose of buttery sweetness. Ambrosial.

Makes about 500g

450g granulated sugar
150ml whole milk
2 tablespoons double cream
75g butter

1 teaspoon glucose powder
$^1/_2$ teaspoon vanilla essence

METHOD

1. Get your food mixer ready – if you have a Kenwood mixer, the K beater works best. Put all the ingredients into a saucepan and, starting on a low heat, gradually bring it up to the boil, stirring as you do so to bring the ingredients together. You are waiting for the mixture to reach the 'soft ball' stage. One of the best ways of judging this is the old-fashioned technique: set aside a bowl filled with cold water and drop in a small blob of the fudge mixture; when it is ready it should be kneadable between your finger and thumb and feel like a 'soft ball'. The more scientific among us should note that this 'soft ball' stage occurs at 116°C.
2. When the mix reaches 'soft ball', pour it into the mixer bowl and beat furiously. This is the tricky part and you must concentrate – the instant the mix starts to pull together as a smooth fudge, stop beating! If you go on for even a few seconds your fudge will turn into an intractable lump.
3. Pour the fudge into a tray and cool. When it has solidified, cut into fudge-sized pieces and store in an airtight container.

THE BEEKEEPER'S APPRENTICE

WORCESTERSHIRE

THERE'S SOMETHING MYSTICAL and magical about bees. Setting aside the cornucopia of different honeys – each jar full of sunlight and preserving the flavours of a particular time and place – bees are organised, logical insects who build works of art in wax and do mankind an immense favour by pollinating fruit and flowers. All of which makes it more disturbing that there is a growing problem in the ranks of beekeepers: as elderly beekeepers retire or buzz off to that great apiary in the sky, we need more novices to step forward.

Lucy Harris is an exception. With her husband Paul she runs a smallholding and bed and breakfast in an elegant Grade II listed farmhouse in Worcestershire. For several years a beekeeper from Worcester had kept his hives in the Harris's orchard, but in the end he found that he no longer had the time or inclination to visit his outlying bees and asked if Lucy would like to take them over. Mrs Harris is a capable, organised sort of person who never does anything by halves (her well regarded B&B gets four diamonds from the 'Farmstay' programme) and she set herself the task of learning about beekeeping. Even in our technological age, beekeeping is still more of an art than a science and for the novice a hundred worries jostle to head the list. What about swarms? Do you get stung? Where do you get practical experience? Are the bees going to mean hours of work every week? Will the garden end up full of crazed killer insects?

As befits an area that includes many large orchards, beekeeping has deep foundations in Worcestershire. On 14 October 1882, a meeting was held in the Guildhall that proposed the establishment of a Worcestershire Beekeeping Association. From the minutes we can see that in seconding the motion Dr Fernie said that in his busy professional life, if he could run to his bees for half an hour he found inexhaustible delight. A Mr Huckle gave several instances of profitable beekeeping – a railway signalman who had made £30 from selling honey in a single year, while a cottager in Hertfordshire harvested over 1000lb of honey from just 14 skeps. The meeting was chaired by the Reverend J. Ross Barker who summed things up... beekeeping was not always a success but it was a source of interest and cultivated the intelligence. The motion was carried.

Fast forward to the twenty-first century: a man called Martyn Cracknell has taken over from Doctor Fernie and the Reverend and each autumn – aided and abetted by his wife Cheryl – he runs a ten-week course in beekeeping. You pitch up one evening a week and during the first weeks cover all the theory as well as practical stuff like assembling honey frames and the construction of a hive. The last two classes are practical, with real bees, and the tyro beekeepers get to see whether they are suited to the art before they have to splash out on their own equipment like the all-important beekeeper's veil. For over a decade the Cracknells have inspired a steady flow of beginners taking their first steps towards beekeeping.

In the Victorian era beekeeping was central to the life of country people, as the signalman would confirm it was a handy source of income, but in those days there was a seemingly inexhaustible supply of wild bees, so much so that it was common practice to empty the hives each autumn so as to avoid the chore of keeping the bees through the winter. Then in the spring it was simply a matter of gathering one of the plentiful wild swarms to provide honey for the year. Would that it were so simple to start beekeeping in the modern era.

Honeybees are under a great deal of pressure. On the one hand farmers continue to make the job of growing food into a more and more inflexible and industrial process and on the other there have been a series of plagues that have targeted the bee. Trapped between the ravages of indiscriminate spraying of insecticides; attacks from the varroa mite; and the sinister sounding 'colony collapse disorder' – a kind of Marie Celeste affair, whereby the beekeeper opens the hive one morning to find that the bees (or 90 per cent of them) have vanished – our bees are on the back foot. The doomsday consequences of wiping out pollinating insects should be obvious, and it's not as if the honeybee is the only pollinator under threat, bumblebee numbers are also nosediving.

This is where Martyn Cracknell and Lucy Harris (and a few hundred like-minded souls scattered across Britain) are stepping up to the plate. We need more beekeepers. There are people whose business is bees – the 'bee farmers' who run commercial honey operations and take fees from enlightened farmers to move their hives into orchards and fields during the pollination season – but the small scale hobbyist beekeepers with as few as two hives have an equally important role to play.

There is a common misconception that to keep bees you need to live in the country and to have rolling acres or at the very least an orchard; in fact, bees that live in town gardens tend to produce more honey – the garden flowers and trees surrounding the hive prove a more profitable hunting ground for nectar and pollen than the barren fields of agribusiness.

Non-beekeepers have an irrational fear of being stung, but beekeepers know that bees vary from colony to colony. Martyn Cracknell has spent a lifetime carefully breeding out the undesirable traits. As he puts it, 'You can have Labrador bees or Rottweiler bees. When he was younger my son fell out of an apple tree on top of a bee hive. He was shaken, and so were the bees, but he didn't get stung. I aim for benign bees.' If the prospect of bee stings is all that is preventing you from keeping bees, take heart. When asked how often he gets stung Martyn reckons that during the course of a year (in which he works with the bees for several hours each week) he may end up getting stung seven or eight times, but over the years he has built up some immunity. And if all the tales of bee stings being the 'magic bullet' when it comes to treating arthritis are true, he is looking forward to a more comfortable old age than the rest of us.

There's a lot of folklore about bees and beekeepers – tales of having to go to the bees and tell them whenever there is a birth or a death in the family – but it seems likely that this may have been a backhanded way to encourage beekeepers to look at their bees regularly. Martyn Cracknell insists that by listening to the noise the bees are making you can gauge their mood. Sometimes it's a lazy and indulgent hum and on another occasion it might be a busier buzz. When asked whether he talks to his bees, Martyn doesn't immediately dismiss the idea, but he does add that he also talks to all manner of inanimate objects! There is something very soothing about bees, which is doubtless why so many have written of the soporific hum of contented bees being the sound of summer. Martyn Cracknell is more prosaic: 'There is a great advantage in having private time with your bees. With the veil on you cannot get at your mobile phone. Nothing disturbs you, you are looking into their world.' Keeping bees is the epitome of working with nature rather than against it. In order to get started Lucy Harris first went on the beekeepers course run by the Cracknells and then got in touch with her local beekeepers' association. They provided her with her first swarm of bees and a 'mentor' – someone she could turn to when she had problems. Beekeepers are a tightly knit group, but unfailingly helpful. Even if beekeeping had less impeccable environmental credentials it would still be worth doing for the honey. Setting aside the currently fashionable arguments for dosing yourself with local honey (and thus local pollens) as a way of avoiding the worst symptoms of hay fever; and the almost magical antiseptic properties of manuka honey – the Tregothnan Estate in Cornwall has started planting manuka bushes so that they can produce an English manuka honey – there is a honey to suit everyone. Because honey reflects the nectar the bees were feeding on, different honeys have different characteristics – when made from raspberry flowers, or oilseed rape, the honey will be high in glucose, which makes it crystallise very quickly and with a fine grain. But honey made from lime blossom tends to be higher in fructose so it will taste sweeter and be slower to granulate with coarse crystals. And as a consequence of the higher fructose levels lime blossom honey will have a significantly lower glycaemic index than glucose heavy honeys.

Two things must happen if we are to avert disaster. The first step would be for farmers to start acknowledging the value of bees. Much of Britain's farmland is in the hands of large agribusinesses and the working of the land is delegated to contractors. These contractors should start by following the directions relating to agrichemicals. Most sprays carry specific directions about where, and in what season, they may be used, even stipulating weather conditions and at what time of day they should be applied. The law also calls for a spray-free six-metre buffer zone around each field. Sometimes these rules are followed but sometimes they are ignored in the rush to get a job done. Cheryl Cracknell found herself arguing with a tractor driver enthusiastically spraying insecticide on crops at noon, on a hot day, in the fields next door to the hives. He politely referred her to the farm manager, who was elsewhere and whose mobile was turned off. Then he carried on spraying. Fortunately the Cracknells' bees were foraging elsewhere, but it only takes a single lapse to annihilate a colony. It's most unlikely that any bumblebees or other pollinators escaped unscathed.

The other hope for the future is you! Get yourself some pollination pets, a couple of hives would be happy in your garden, especially if you live in a town – there are productive beehives on the roof of Fortnum & Mason, the food store on Piccadilly in London. Get in touch with your local branch of the British Beekeepers' Association and ask for help with the first steps, then sit back and imagine your own natural golden honey dripping off the edge of a thick slice of hot buttered toast.

DINNER WITH

ANNIE STAGG AND HOLLIBERRY

WINCANTON, SOMERSET

WHEN I FIRST RANG ANNIE STAGG she was in the woods near Stavordale Priory with her beloved blue and tan Border terrier Holliberry and they were busy gathering the last of the wild garlic leaves to make soup. Annie has lived in London, East Anglia and Amsterdam, but now divides her time between London – working with a law firm in south London – and Wincanton, where things run at a gentler pace. Her love of cooking came about via osmosis; her grandfather was a gamekeeper in Scotland and when she visited him she absorbed his credo that it was wrong to shoot any animals unless they were going to end up in the pot. He was also a firm believer in seasonal and wild food which gave Annie a lifetime love of foraging. As befits someone passionate about cooking Annie has been on a number of courses, but in the end she finds herself coming back to the classic books – Mrs Beeton and Alexis Soyer are two favourites.

As you enter Annie's kitchen you can see that this is a place where cooking is taken seriously, there is an orderly 'get-down-to-business' air to the place. The cookbooks get their own large shelf, but the heart of the matter is a small and crammed card index stuffed with recipes written out carefully in neat handwriting. You get the feeling that precision is important and attention to detail mandatory. The other thing that quickly becomes apparent is her unflagging loyalty to seasonal food and local produce.

The dinner menu reflected all these principles. The starter is a 'ravioli' of Cornish crab with a kaffir lime leaf sauce – even a gentle tease that the Cornish crab might not be indigenous to south-eastern Somerset is met with a straight bat – she has chosen Cornish crab because they are in such good condition at this time of year.

The second course is a magnificent cut of veal. Annie has chosen the eye of the sirloin, arguing that it has more flavour than the fillet. This was cooked simply, crisply sizzled outside and juicy within, and it came with a rich and creamy green peppercorn sauce and fresh vegetables – the newest new potatoes, young carrots, all the herbs and vegetables coming from her, or her neighbours', gardens.

Annie gets her veal from nearby Kimbers' Farm, which is something of a local institution; the farm on Blackmore Vale has been in the Kimber family for over 300 years. The current generation, Paul and Ruth Kimber, run the place on old-fashioned lines as a mixed stock farm, which means that there is fine veal to be had. Let's be clear, this is rose veal and the calves are allowed to suckle from their mothers, see the sun and enjoy the grass. It's a long way from the pallid white meat from Continental veal farms, where calves are fed milk while being kept in crates and sometimes deprived of light – anything to ensure that the meat ends up almost white. Proper veal is pink and juicy, it also has a rich and satisfying taste, which means you can cook it simply but still enjoy it. We should all be eating more British veal, at least anyone who drinks milk should make a point of demanding it. The industrialisation of our dairy industry means that in Britain thousands of calves are born every day, because until she has calved the sensible cow doesn't produce milk. Natural laws then take a hand ensuring that half of these babies are male calves – not much good for producing milk – which means that pure economics often doom them to being killed at birth. If we were to establish a larger market for rose veal, those male calves could all be grown on with their mothers.

Nothing changes a farmer's attitudes quite so briskly as being offered a decent price for his animals.

The dessert was a double-barrelled delight, on the one hand an über-rich chocolate cake and on the other a passion fruit brûléed tart. When asked to choose, the only sensible response was 'Both please!'

CRAB RAVIOLI WITH A KAFFIR LIME LEAF SAUCE

These are not really ravioli but they are very delicious. Annie uses fresh Cornish crab and 'cheats' by buying dumpling wrappers – the result is a very delicate skin and a great deal less effort. Annie gets her 'gyoza wrappers' from a Korean supermarket in New Malden, south London – they are much less work, and cheap too!

Serves 4 (makes 24 ravioli)

1 packet of 48 dumpling wrappers
1 egg white
a few large prawns, butterflied (optional)

For the poaching liquid and sauce
300ml tub supermarket fish stock
175ml double cream
6 kaffir lime leaves, finely shredded

For the filling
250g fresh crab meat (white only)
2 tablespoons crème fraîche
a handful of finely chopped fresh dill
1 teaspoon finely grated fresh ginger root
1 flat teaspoon wasabi (or a finely chopped hot chilli if your prefer)

METHOD

1. First, prepare the poaching liquid. Combine the fish stock with the cream in a deep frying pan. Add the kaffir lime leaves, stir and heat through. Set aside to infuse.
2. Next, make the filling: take a large bowl and mix the crab meat, crème fraîche, nearly all the dill, the ginger and wasabi. If you like things spicy, add a little more wasabi or abandon it in favour of chopped fresh hot chilli.
3. Lay out 24 of the dumpling wraps; place a small dollop of the mixture in the centre of each. Brush the periphery with egg white, place another wrapper on top and pinch the edges together, making sure that you get a good seal. You can make the ravioli ahead of time; just lay them out on a tray in the fridge until needed.
4. Heat the poaching liquid to just under boiling point, slide the ravioli into the pan and simmer until the pastry is cooked –3–5 minutes depending how crowded they are. You may need to do this in batches.
5. Divide the ravioli between hot soup bowls. Allow six per person and keep them warm while you reduce the poaching liquid to make the sauce. It should end up thick enough to coat the back of a wooden spoon. Check the seasoning and adjust if necessary. Spoon over. Dress with the remaining chopped dill. You can add some large prawns by way of garnish if you wish.

SIRLOIN OF VEAL WITH A CREAM AND GREEN PEPPERCORN SAUCE

The cooking of the veal is very simple and the making of the sauce very arduous – not surprising as the key ingredient is a vegetable and herb stock.

Serves 4

For the stock
1 large onion, chopped
1 leek, sliced
2 celery sticks, sliced
1 fennel bulb, chopped into 1cm cubes
4 large carrots, sliced
1 garlic bulb, sliced horizontally
12 peppercorns, crushed
1 teaspoon fresh green peppercorns
1 teaspoon coriander seeds
1 star anise
1 bay leaf
50g fresh mixed garden herbs
1.5 litres cold water
300ml dry white wine

For the green peppercorn sauce
600ml vegetable stock
200g unsalted butter, chilled and diced
1 teaspoon fresh lemon juice
1 teaspoon fresh green peppercorns
100ml double cream
salt and freshly ground black pepper

For the veal
clarified butter (you could use ghee)
4 pieces English rose veal, each about 10x5cm
and at least 4cm thick, lean and tender (ask
your butcher for the eye of the sirloin)

METHOD

1. Two days ahead of time, make the stock. Put all the ingredients except the wine into a large saucepan, bring to simmering point (just below boiling point) and simmer for 10 minutes. Remove from the heat and stir in the wine. Cover and leave in a cool place for 48 hours. Strain through a sieve; you should have 1.2 litres vegetable stock. You will only use half of this in the sauce; the remainder can be frozen for another occasion.

2. On the day, make the green peppercorn sauce. Reduce the stock in a heavy pan over a high heat. You are aiming to reduce it by four-fifths. When the volume is down to a fifth of what it was it will be thick and sticky.

3. Reduce the heat and whisk in the cubes of cold butter a little at a time (you can use a hand-held blender to do this if you prefer). As the butter melts it will thicken up

the sauce and make it glossy. Add the lemon juice and green peppercorns. Keep warm but do not allow to boil.

4. In another large pan bring the cream to the boil, then add the stock and butter mix, whisking as you go – the sauce should never boil again. Season to taste before serving.

5. Finally, prepare the veal. Heat a little clarified butter in a pan and fry the veal, pressing it down and turning regularly to ensure browning. It's a matter of taste but English veal responds well to being served when juicy. Press down on the meat and it should feel firm and springy when properly cooked, this should take about 10 minutes. Serve with the green peppercorn sauce and fresh vegetables.

MOSQUETOIRS NEARLY FLOURLESS CHOCOLATE CAKE

The origin of this recipe is Annie's fabled card index, before that it was sighted in a long-forgotten magazine and before that it came from France – hence the name. Choice of chocolate is very important as it is imperative that the finished cake doesn't end up over-sweet. Annie uses those cylindrical packs of Venezuelan Black chocolate from Willie Harcourt-Cooze of television fame, but any dark chocolate that contains over 70 per cent cocoa solids will suffice.

Serves 8

For the cake	1 tablespoon plain flour
200g dark chocolate, minimum 70% cocoa solids	
175g hazelnuts	*For the frosting*
4 large eggs, separated	200g dark chocolate, minimum 70% cocoa solids
150g unsalted butter, softened	3 tablespoons golden syrup
175g caster sugar	75g unsalted butter

METHOD

1. Preheat the oven to 180°C (170°C if a fan oven)/350°F/gas mark 4. Line a 20cm wide, deep, loose-bottomed cake tin with baking parchment. Melt the chocolate gently in a bain-marie (or a bowl over simmering water, but be careful that the bowl doesn't touch the water).

2. Toast the hazelnuts and then grind them up in a blender, but not too savagely; you need crumbs not powder.
3. Cream the egg yolks, butter and sugar together using a mixer. Beat well until it is very pale. Cool the chocolate a little and work it into the egg yolk mixture. Stir in the hazelnuts and the flour.
4. In a separate bowl, whisk the egg whites to soft peaks. Fold the chocolate mixture into the egg white mix, working gently to retain as much air as possible. Pour into the tin, banging it down on the work surface to eliminate air pockets. Bake in the centre of the oven for 40–50 minutes – when it is done, a palette knife slipped into the heart of the cake will come out clean.
5. Cool for 10 minutes in the tin, then turn out onto a cooling rack.
6. To make the frosting, melt the chocolate as for the cake and stir in the syrup. Remove from the heat, add the butter and beat as it cools, until it becomes 'spreadable'. Spread this over the cake, which should be cold to the touch by now. Leave the surface rough – 'forked'. Serve cut into slices with clotted cream.

BOMA'S BRÛLÉED PASSION FRUIT TART

Annie collected this recipe from the cook at the Boma guest house in Uganda.
You can vary the amount of pastry used to arrive at the perfect thickness for the
particular flan tin you are using. In an ideal world the pastry for the finished tart
should start 5mm thick and end up thin and crisp.

Serves 8

For the pastry case	For the filling
350g plain flour	10 passion fruit (you need about 200ml purée)
175g caster sugar	4 eggs
200g butter, cut into small cubes	200g caster sugar
1 lemon	225ml double cream
a little cold water	remaining juice from the lemon (opposite)
	50g icing sugar

METHOD

1. First make the pastry case. Preheat the oven to 180°C/350°F/gas mark 4. Place
   the flour, sugar and butter in a food processor and whizz until the mixture
   resembles breadcrumbs. Add a squeeze of lemon juice, then gradually add some
   cold water, continuously pulsing the mixture, until the dough comes together in
   a ball. Wrap in clingfilm and rest in the fridge for at least 1 hour.
2. Grease a 25cm loose-bottomed flan tin. Roll out the pastry and use to line the tin.
   Add some baking parchment and beans to weigh it down during blind baking.
   Bake for 20 minutes. Remove from the oven, remove the parchment and beans
   and leave to cool. Reduce the oven to 160°C/325°F/gas mark 3.
3. Scoop out the insides of the passion fruit. You want some seeds (but not too many)
   in the final tart, so put the pulp from 2 fruit straight into a large mixing bowl and
   then push the remaining fruit through a sieve.
4. Beat the eggs and sugar together until they are fluffy, add the cream, then the
   passion fruit purée and lemon juice. Whisk together and pour into the cooked
   case. Cover the pastry edges with foil to stop them charring and bake for
   30 minutes until set. Keep an eye on the tart during the later stages of cooking.
5. Sprinkle the surface with icing sugar and brûlée – either with a kitchen blow
   lamp or under a fierce grill – until crisp and glassy.

KING OF PIGS

SOMERSET

TAMWORTH PIGS ARE CHARMING CREATURES, they will look you in the eye, smile and then do whatever they choose. Showing any pig is a difficult job; the idea is that the pigs walk gently round the ring at an agricultural show while the judge – usually a weather-beaten fellow in a bowler hat or a resolute lady with the kind of floral headgear usually reserved for country weddings – decides whether the hams are perfect; whether the underline is sufficiently elegant; and if the head is carried well while also considering a host of other arcane porcine beauty traits. The pig's minder (or minders – boars must have two handlers in the showing ring) has an old walking stick and a board for steering, you block off the left-hand side of the pig's head with the board, then he or she obediently turns to the right in order to see round the obstruction. So far, so good. Pig showing is a pleasant country ritual that's as much a part of summer as the hum of a bumblebee. Lean on the arena fence and watch a dozen large, plump pigs amble round the ring snuffling to themselves. Then it's time for a rude awakening as the Tamworth class storms into the ring.

In the main Tamworths are larger than their handlers, quicker than their handlers, and dangerously clever. Imagine you were trying out your stick and board pig guidance techniques on a large, ginger sofa fitted with an outboard motor – bulky but athletic and with an impressive turn of speed. Sensibly enough, Nick Hunkin now concentrates on commentating at the shows and spends more time with microphone in hand than he does chivvying his beloved Tammys. Each year his Shutevale herd of pedigree Tamworths racks up an impressive tally of championships and interbreed cups after the animals have been paraded round the ring by Nick's raggle-taggle army of teenage helpers. The deal is that if the kids help with the work in the piggery, Nick will take them away to the shows all expenses paid. It's one time when like seems to cancel out like, both the teenagers and the Tamworths are frisky, flighty and out for a good time. The showing season is one long party for them all.

Showing would be a good deal easier if the pigs were not so bright. Nick still tells a tale from the early days – at one of the first shows on the calendar, the Devon County perhaps – a competing sow sidled up to Shutevale Melody 3rd and bit her in the bum. Shutevale etcetera, who was generally known as Henrietta, limped on out of sorts and ended up with a rather depressing fourth place. But such is the perspicacity of Tammys that at the far end of the long showing season, Henrietta found herself entering the ring at the Newbury Show, and caught sight of her old adversary. She abandoned her handler, rushed across the arena and bit her rival in the hams. On that occasion the enemy was limping while Henrietta secured the championship she deserved.

Nick Hunkin is the son of a Devon farmer and in the 1950s and 1960s delighted in what he now describes as the heyday of the small mixed farm, 'when the farmer worked with Nature rather than against it'. The Hunkins kept a few dairy cattle, a few beef cattle, some sheep and some saddleback pigs. They grew a bit of corn. They lovingly tended the ancient meadows and were rewarded by impressive milk yields. Towards the end of the 1960s things started to change. The pigs had to go, then the sheep and beef steers had to go as the dairy herd grew and the word 'intensive' started to be bandied around in farming circles. Finally, as with so many other farming families, the Hunkins hit the buffers. Nick wanted to take over the farm from his father while his two sisters and mother were all for selling up. The ladies got their way and Nick moved to London and a job as an auctioneer. It wasn't long before the people who bought the farm brought in the most valuable crop of them all – an estate of executive houses. Talking about it still upsets Nick, 'I try not to drive past the old place as I don't like seeing the best meadows under concrete.'

Fast forward a decade and a Show and Sale run by the Devon branch of the Rare Breeds Survival Trust, in Exeter – one of the lots was an elegant Tamworth gilt, 'Gilhouse Lucky Lass 37th'. Before he could convince his wife that they needed a pig; before he had convinced the seller that he had anywhere to keep a pig, let alone any way of transporting her home, Nick had bought her. That pig, aka 'Poppy', was to be the foundation of the Shutevale herd. What could so easily have been a lesson in the wisdom of sitting on your hands while at an auction eventually turned out rather well. Some neighbours had an old piggery they were prepared to rent out and Nick managed to borrow an old Bedford van to take Poppy home. 'The journey wasn't too bad, we put some straw bales across behind the front seats and she couldn't quite reach the steering wheel with her nose.' Later that summer Poppy won the Tamworth championship at the Okehampton show, much to the delight of her sceptical breeder who could now tell by the splendid condition of the champion that Nick had a real talent for pig keeping. 'In the beginning I think the lady who bred Poppy thought I was some green-wellied man from Godalming, it was difficult persuading her I could be trusted with a Tamworth, especially as at the time I had nowhere to keep one.'

If you ask Nick Hunkin why he has been such a fervent supporter of Tamworth pigs he goes all sheepish and will give you a long rambling speech about the importance of preserving rare breeds. The truth is he fell in love with Poppy. When he was starting out in Tammys, the breed was in a parlous situation: the 'intensive' farming imperatives of the 1980s meant that pigs needed to be long-backed, white-skinned and docile, so numbers of the huge, independently-minded ginger pigs were declining fast.

Nick's pig-keeping ambitions took a turn for the better when he was lucky enough to find a smallholding owned by the Somerset County Council – 2½ acres, a barn and a few old stables. He took it on and now the Shutevale herd had a headquarters and room for expansion. Over the roller-coaster years and through two bouts of foot and mouth disease, the number of pigs at his piggery has varied enormously. Pigs are busy animals and each year every sow has two litters, which can mean as many as thirty-two piglets. Sows need a boar, and the herd needs a young boar in training, so to enter a few pig shows with some gilts, and a junior boar plus a senior sow and boar means that your dozen travelling superstars represent a much larger herd. They really are the best of the best.

Before the Second World War pig showing was a vital part of the agricultural economy, but often a stockman's livelihood depended on winning – in the 1930s a prize boar could fetch £1,000 (which is equivalent to a modern-day £15,000 to £20,000!). No wonder there are well documented cases of pigmen sleeping with their charges during the night before the competition to avoid 'pig-knobbling'. Pigs are sensitive creatures and waking them up abruptly in the middle of the night is enough to impair their performance in the show the following day. Nick insists that there are dark mutterings about present-day pig knobblers who are alleged to try everything from squirting water into a sow's ear (that will make her shake her head for the following day and walk round the ring unbalanced with her head on one side) to the altogether more beastly 'drawing pin in the trotter' to make her lame.

For the Chairman of the Tamworth Breeder's Club Nick is remarkably tolerant of other breeds and has 'dabbled' in Oxford Sandy and Blacks, Middlewhites and, most surprising of all, Landrace. It seems odd that someone so passionate about rare breeds would give houseroom to a commercial pig like the Landrace. If you ask him why he started to keep a commercial pig like Landrace he will respond with a short lecture on their origins. The breed was developed by the Danes in the 1930s and its ancestors include eight different traditional British pigs. But as pig farming became more and more intensive in the 1980s, 'closed unit' piggeries adopted more and more stringent hygiene policies, culminating in an edict which meant that any pig leaving the premises could never return and must be slaughtered. This Draconian approach put an end to showing and any interchange of stock putting gene diversity at risk. As ever, Nick ended up keeping Landrace pigs for the good of the pigs!

The mathematics of pig-keeping is awe-inspiring. Even with a small herd the sows produce a remarkable number of pigs per year. Each that ends up in the herd book gets a three-part name. For example 'Shutevale' (that's the herd), 'Lucky Lass' (that part comes from her mother or his father), and finally the 750th – signifying that this pig is the 750th born of that line in this particular herd. And yes, the numbers of Shutevale pedigree Tamworth sows has already passed 750. These figures mask a good deal of heartache. Pig food is pricy so sentiment must take second place to decisive action. It makes sense to grow the litter on a bit before deciding on any potential champions but any pig breeder always has more boars than he needs, and some farmers are forced to shoot surplus piglets as soon as they are born.

If you ask Nick his favourite cut of pork he responds with the alacrity of a true enthusiast: his loyalties are split between a roast loin of pork (well-fatted for great crackling) and the perfect bacon sandwich (streaky bacon cooked until very crisp indeed and doughy white bread). If you then ask him what it's like to eat a pig he's brought up he looks at you rather blankly, like everyone with farming in their blood he has an inbuilt pragmatism. Without the ongoing cycle of breeding there would be no superstar show pigs; waste and cruelty are unacceptable and so each month another batch of weaners go off to the fatteners and thence to slaughter. This philosophy extends to sows and boars that are growing old – as soon as they falter there is no alternative but to send them to the slaughterhouse where they can be dispatched humanely.

In the final analysis Nick Hunkin keeps pigs for two reasons, one practical and one sentimental. On the practical side he points out that in the 20th century animal fat has become a public enemy whereas in the 19th century, when there was no central heating and much more work was manual, it was a vital component of any sensible diet. We just don't know what the future holds and there may come a time when we will need the attributes of rare breed animals: hardiness; higher fat levels; better mothering skills. If the Tamworth gene pool were to be lost we would have no way of recovering it. How could anyone be so careless as to stand by while we lose such a valuable resource? Nick's second argument for Tammys is more sentimental, he points out that we spend huge sums preserving stately homes, antiques and sites of special scientific interest, surely livestock has equal merit. He sees the bold ginger pig that is the children's favourite and has come down to us from Iron Age times as living history and something that demands our support.

Sadly, 2009 saw the last Royal Show. This was the 160th year that the Royal Agricultural Society of England had run what was the most prestigious event on the farming calendar. Standing by the Main Ring as the last ever Grand Parade of cattle snaked around the arena brought a tear to the eye – so many magnificent animals, so many breeds, what an advertisement for British Farming. The parade of cattle took over 30 minutes to wind past – from Dexters to Holsteins to White Park cattle and ruby red Devons. What a tragedy it is that farming has lost this showcase. Down at the pig lines, however, things were less melancholy. Over the years Nick Hunkin has had several champions at the Royal – large whites and middle whites, but never his beloved Tamworths. But, at the last ever Royal Show, Shutevale Lucky Lass 761 won the Tamworth Championship and the magnificent Rufforth Perpetual Challenge Cup. Congratulations to the King of pigs! Talk about leaving it to the last minute.

LUNCH WITH
CAROLINE AND MARK
TETLEY
GRAMPOUND, CORNWALL

THE TREES ARE OLD AND GNARLED and rooted in mossy banks, the branches meet overhead and as you turn up the drive between the soldier-straight ancient stone gateposts it is like entering a viridian green tunnel. While in the rest of Britain the manor houses tend to be built on the high ground with commanding views, in Cornwall things are different. Here the bigger houses nestle into the deep valleys trying to shelter their occupants from the wind. The surrounding fields are plush and the stock are sleek, but it doesn't take a lot of imagination to see that even down here in the balmy south-west the cold winter months would have teeth.

Mark and Caroline Tetley live in a converted coach house with their children George and Dido – as well as a snaking row of Wellington boots outside the door there's a drying room and a practical farmhouse kitchen complete with an Aga. As most of the farm work on the estate is contracted out, Mark has time for a day job and each week he makes the trek to London to work in the City. Food and cookery enjoys a gratifyingly high priority in this household: fifteen-year-old Dido keeps pigs – a happy, rootling Large Black sow and her litter charge inquisitively across the paddock to greet you. Carrying a bucket always makes you best friends with any kind of livestock and these cheerful piggies haven't realised that some of them will probably end up as Christmas presents – a Yuletide ham from the Tetley family is highly prized in this part of Cornwall. George Tetley, Caroline's older brother, keeps large and beautiful Sussex chickens and switches from talking about their showing potential to their role as the heart of a coq au vin with no sign of irony. He is concerned that having built them a palatial chicken house atop a tall pole with a fox-unfriendly ladder to climb up to roost (à la Hugh Fearnley-Whittingstall) the burly fowl refuse to ascend at bedtime. He also keeps quail and finds them much easier to care for. George also asks for advice on another project: marinating in a range of bowls on the kitchen worktop are the ingredients for the S.P.Q.R. terrine he is trying to perfect – that's squirrel, pheasant, quail and rabbit! The problem is one of judging the cooking time with such varied ingredients.

Caroline is a capable and organised cook, she has no time for lofty airs and graces, 'I'm not an adventurous cook, I do what I know I can do. But it's very encouraging that our children and their friends are so interested in cooking.' There is a very topical and modernist feel to the Tetley's kitchen economy. The primary source of food is close at hand – vegetables come from the raised beds in the garden and the greenhouse; pork, bacon and sausages come from the Large Blacks; game from the shoot; eggs from the hens, guinea fowl and quail; fruit from the fruit trees. What's more, common sense and recycling seem to be the guiding principles by which they live – everything from vegetable trimmings to windfalls and stale bread get used up as pig food. As Caroline puts it, 'We tend to use home produce whenever we can, and try not to waste leftovers, it may sound a bit like wartime frugality but it is a good feeling.'

Discussion at lunch ranges from sailing (a family passion) to food, ingredients, cooking and food. The meal is one of those jolly meandering affairs. To start with we have a 'Summer soup' – a gentle tomatoey soup served cold with lots of added extras: crisp croutons of fried bread; slices of nutty black olives; tiny cubes of red pepper. It's mix and match, rather like one of those old-fashioned Raj-style curries where legion side dishes overwhelm the main dish. The main course is sausages in cider, and it is a genuine rib-sticker. It helps that the sausages are made from Dido's porkers, and it helps that Caroline and the butcher are in cahoots – these bangers are made from shoulder, belly, and the cheek meat with a little rusk and a seasoning of black pepper and garlic. A very good sausage indeed. They end up in a casserole with a topping of fried apples. Pudding is a serious affair – rich, sugary and buttery, the 'pear and ginger upside-down cake' is turned out on a plate in all its sticky glory to wait for a melting dollop of Cornish clotted cream.

There is a charming simplicity to Caroline's cookery. Nothing is pretentious. Nothing is fussily presented. Flavours are on the button. These dishes have integrity and balance and they are very good to eat.

SUMMER SOUP

This is a cold soup that ends up smooth and tomatoey, very refreshing. By way of a counterpoint it is served with a range of different 'sprinkles' that add crunch and zing. Summer soup is easy to make but somewhat laborious, the time you save by not skinning and deseeding the tomatoes is balanced out by the need to push the purée through a sieve.

Serves 6

1.2 kg ripe tomatoes	120ml extra virgin olive oil
4 slices white bread, crusts removed	4 tablespoons mayonnaise
2 cucumbers, roughly chopped	(shop bought is fine)
1 large sweet Spanish onion, sliced	750ml tomato juice (you can use V8 if
1 clove of garlic, peeled	you prefer)
2 tablespoons red wine vinegar	salt and freshly ground black pepper

METHOD

1. Put the tomatoes in the food processor and whizz until liquid. Push through a sieve (leaving behind the skins and seeds) into a big bowl.
2. Whizz the bread, cucumbers, onion, garlic, vinegar, oil, mayonnaise and tomato juice together until very smooth. Mix both purées together and season to taste.
3. Serve with a range of 'sprinkles'. Pick any or all of the following: fried bread croutons; crispy bacon pieces; sliced olives; red peppers (in small dice); shredded green chillies. Do not float ice cubes in this soup unless (a) we are enjoying a tropical heatwave or (b) you like watery soup..

SAUSAGES IN CIDER

It is a general rule that sausages are only ever as good as you make them. It sounds self-evident but when butchers lavish care and attention on their sausages, making them with the best bits of pork belly and shoulder, you get a better class of banger than when they are the repository for all the unhappy scraps of meat that cannot otherwise be sold. The Tetleys' sausages are notable, and so they should be, as they are made by a local butcher using pork from the sleek Large Black pigs belonging to Dido, the daughter of the house. We ate 'garlic and black pepper' sausages and very good they were too.

Serves 6

40g unsalted butter
18 good-quality pork sausages
350g thick-cut back bacon
400g button onions or shallots, peeled but
left whole
1 garlic clove, crushed

1 tablespoon flour
330ml cider
2 bay leaves
freshly ground black pepper
3 dessert apples

METHOD

1. Preheat the oven to 180°C/350°F/gas mark 4. Use half the butter to fry the sausages quickly until golden brown. Lift them out with tongs and transfer to a large, heavy casserole.
2. Chop the bacon into small pieces and fry in the remaining fat. Add the bacon to the pot and fry the whole onions until they colour, then add the garlic. Stir well and add to the casserole.
3. Sprinkle the flour into the casserole. Pour over the cider then add the bay leaves and a good twist of freshly ground black pepper; the seasoning of the sausages and bacon should mean that you don't need to add salt. Cover and cook in the oven for 30 minutes. Remove the lid and cook for a further 30 minutes.
4. Immediately before serving, peel, core and slice the apples (the slices should be about 5mm thick) then fry them in the remaining butter until golden brown. Layer across the top of the casserole. Serve with simple mashed potato and a green vegetable.

STICKY PEAR AND GINGER UPSIDE-DOWN PUDDING

Tarte tatin, eat your heart out! Make way for this wildly self-indulgent, very sticky old-fashioned pudding. Introducing the kind of dish that makes you postpone your diet until another day. Serve with Cornish clotted cream in large dollops, or perhaps some thick yellow custard.

Serves 6

50g butter
240g soft brown sugar
1 (400g) tin pear halves
100g stem ginger, chopped into small chunks
125 white flour
pinch of ground cloves
2 teaspoons ground cinnamon
1/2 teaspoon grated nutmeg

2 teaspoons ground ginger
1/2 teaspoon salt
1/2 teaspoon bicarbonate of soda
50g hard vegetable margarine
125ml whole milk
100g black treacle
1 egg

METHOD

1. Preheat the oven to 180°C/350°F/gas mark 4. Melt the butter and half the brown sugar together over a low heat and pour into a 20cm square, deep-sided cake tin.
2. Drain the tinned pears and arrange them in the cake tin (rounded side down). Pop a piece of stem ginger into each cavity and sprinkle the rest across the tin.
3. Put the flour, cloves, cinnamon, nutmeg, ground ginger, plus the remaining sugar, salt and bicarbonate into a food processor and whizz. Melt the margarine and add to the processor with the milk, treacle and egg. Mix thoroughly until you have a smooth batter. Pour the mixture onto the fruit and bake for 40-50 minutes until the cakey upper part is cooked. Turn out onto a flat plate immediately and leave for 10 minutes to cool a little before serving with clotted cream.

SOME USEFUL STUFF

There was a time when any cookery book worth its salt would be peppered with footnotes all linked to a scholarly bibliography. But the information revolution has made such a concept seem rather redundant. These notes are by no means exhaustive but they do pinpoint a few internet links if you are interested in exploring anything further.

Lunch with Rosie and Andrew Gifford

Andrew Gifford's paintings can be found at the John Martin Gallery, 38 Albemarle Street, London
W1S 4JG
tel: 020 7499 1314
www.jmlondon.com

The Wild Man, forager Fergus Drennan

Fergus Drennan
www.wildmanwildfood.com.

The ultimate book for mushroom hunters - *Mushrooms* by Roger Phillips. (published by Macmillan Reference ISBN 978-0330442374)

Also look out for a copy of
Food for Free by Richard Mabey (published by Collins ISBN-13: 978-0002201599)

The Roasters, Jeremy Torz and Steven Mactonia, Union Hand-Roasted Coffee

Union Hand-Roasted Coffee
www.unionroasted.com
www.fairtrade.org.uk

Lunch with Amanda Woodcraft and family

New Under Ten Fishermen's Association

www.nutfa.org

Lunch with Michael Rodham

The oracle for all things beery – www.camra.org.uk

A macrobiotic dinner with Albert Moss and friends

www.macrobiotics.co.uk

www.prostatecancer.org.uk

A practical overview - *Introduction to Macrobiotics* by Oliver Cowmeadow. (published by Thorsons ISBN 978-0722514146)

The Nose, Charlie MacLean – whisky secrets

www.whiskymac.com

World Whisky (published by Dorling Kindersley, edited by Charles Maclean, ISBN-13: 978-1405341721)

Malt Whisky by Charles MacLean (published by Mitchell Beazley, ISBN-13: 978-1405341721)

Charles Maclean's Whisky Tales (published by Little Books , ISBN-13: 978-1904435631)

Lunch with Merlyn Riggs

www.social-sculpture.org

Social Sculpture - What is Art?: Conversation with Joseph Beuys by Joseph Beuys and Volker Harlan. (published by Clairview ISBN-13: 978-1905570072)

The Big Cheese, Juliet Harbutt, founder of the British Cheese Awards

www.thecheeseweb.com

www.finefoodworld.co.uk

Cheese by Juliet Harbutt & Ros Denny (published by Southwater, ISBN-13: 978-1844764815)

Afternoon tea with Barbara Atkins

The place for all those obscure pieces of home baking kit

www.lakeland.co.uk

The Beekeeper's Apprentice, Lucy Harris and Martyn Cracknell

www.farmstay.co.uk

The British Beekeepers' Association

www.britishbee.org.uk

The Evesham Beekeepers' Association

www.eveshambeekeepers.org.uk

Keeping Bees and Making Honey by Alison Benjamin and Brian McCallum (published by David and Charles, ISBN-13: 978-0715328101)

Beekeeping – Inspiration and practical advice for would-be small holders by Andrew Davies (published by Anova in association with the National Trust ISBN 978-184340 418 7)

Dinner with Annie Stag and Holliberry

The Good Veal Guide

www.helenbrowningorganics.co.uk/the_good_veal_guide.phtml

The King of Pigs, Nick Hunkin and his Tamworths

www.tamworthbreedersclub.co.uk

Rare Breeds Survival Trust , www.rbst.org.uk

Lunch with Caroline and Mark Tetley

Your own sausages - Home Sausage Making by Susan Mahnke Peery and Charles G. Reavis (published by Storey Books; 3rd edition, ISBN 978-1580174718)

IN GENERAL

My own site:
www.charlescampion.com

Kyle Cathie
www.kylecathie.com

Action Against Hunger
www.actionagainsthunger.org

Oxford Gastronomica at Brookes University
www.oxfordgastronomica.brookes.ac.uk

Slow Food
www.slowfood.org.uk

The Guild of Food Writers
www.gfw.co.uk

INDEX

POSTCRIPT

WHAT FUN. WHAT GOOD FOOD. What unfailingly generous hospitality.
I can report that good cooking is alive and well and that all over Britain people
are quietly going about their business dishing up delicious meals. Their recipes
are inspiring. Their invention is humbling and I hope that you enjoy these dishes
as much as I have.

As with any project thanks are due, but with this venture perhaps that is more true
than ever. As well as thanking the cooks of Britain at the heart of this book there is
the matter of the unsung heroes: the friends and acquaintants, friends of friends,
even friends of friends of friends who have helped guide me around Britain on
this odyssey. You know who you are and if I have left you off the list accept a
grovelling apology.

Margaret Bemand; Ros Choate; Suzanne Davies; Bob & Linda Farrand; Rosie
Halloran; Kaylois Henry; Danny & Tracey Kearns; Tim & Diana Meadows; Ian
& Lindsay Murray; Richard & Janette Price; Chris Smalley; Sheila Thorpe; Lyn
Woodcraft.

Then all that remains is to thank the patient people at Kyle Cathie: Kyle herself,
Judith Hannam, Vicki Murrell, Victoria Scales, Julia Barder. Also Jonathan Gray
for both the book design and the illustrations. Thanks are also due to Muna Reyal
who helped oversee the birth of this project.